RECENT ISSUES CONCERNING VIOLENCE AGIANST WOMEN

It is submitted that the exemption given to marital rape does not satisfy both the criteria laid down in different cases and also not according to the valid classification [illegible] Section 375 of Indian Penal Code makes a classification in terms of the exemption that does not regard forceful sexual intercourse in a marriage as rape.

Right to Life and Personal Liberty[21]

Article 21 of the Constitution provides that no person shall be deprived of his life or personal liberty except according to procedure established by Law. Prior to Maneka Gandhi's decision, Article 21 guaranteed the right to life and personal liberty to citizens only against the arbitrary action of the executive and not from legislative action.[22] But after Maneka Gandhi's decision, Article 21 now protects the right of life and personal liberty not only from executive but from legislative action also.[23] In this case the Court gave a new dimension to Article 21. It was held that the right to live is not merely confined to physical existence but it includes within its ambit the right to live with human dignity. It also includes within its scope the Right to Health as is decided in different cases from time to time.[24] In another case the court held that women also have the right to life and liberty; they also have the right to be respected and treated as equal citizens. Their honour and dignity can not be touched or violated. They also have the right to lead an honourable and peaceful life.[25]

If we make an analysis of this particular Article of the Constitution, then it may be found that the marital exemption clause violates Article 21 of the Constitution as it is against the principle of living with human dignity, honour of the wife concerned as in certain circumstances when she is forced to have sexual intercourse against her will. This situation has been seen in the observation of Justice Saghir Ahmad, he observed that "Unfortunately, a women in our country belongs to a class (or group) of society who are in disadvantageous position on the account of several social barriers and impediments and have, therefore, been victim of tyranny at the hands of men with whom they unfortunately enjoy equal status under the Constitution."[26]

Marital Rape as Cruelty

It will be useful to point out that Section 498 A of Indian Penal Code, 1860 amply covers the cause of victims of marital rape since marital rape is a form of cruelty which is perpetrated by the husband on his wife. The explanation to this Section provides that wilful conduct which is of such a nature as is likely to cause danger to health, whether physical or mental of the women accords ample flexibility to cover the cause of a victim of marital rape. It is however submitted that in spite of the fact that an offender of marital rape can be punished under this Section, the fallout of doing so would amount to compromising on realization of reality that rape does happen within private sphere of marriage. Reading rape in to Section 498A would amount to still recognizing the fact of

RECENT ISSUES CONCERNING VIOLENCE AGIANST WOMEN

Edited by

Subhash Chandra Singh

SERIALS PUBLICATIONS
NEW DELHI (INDIA)

First Published - 2011

ISBN: 978-81-8387-472-4

Published by

SERIALS PUBLICATIONS
4830/24, Prahlad Street, Ansari Road
Darya Ganj, New Delhi-110002 (India)
Phone : 23245225 Fax : 91-11-23272135
E-mail: serials@sify.com

CONTENTS

PREFACE

The present book contains eighteen scholarly research papers primarily devoted to the ever increasing problem of domestic violence against women which is a violation of basic human rights to women. All these articles are written by subject experts/specialists who are holding commanding positions in teaching and research educational institutions in India and abroad. The articles have wide range of subject and circulation in the world through "Indian Journal of Human Rights and Justice" which is distributed by M/s Serial Publications, Darya Ganj, New Delhi. But the idea behind publication of these articles is to present relevant reading material on the subject at one place for the convenience of the research scholars and general readers in the libraries.

Violence against women and girls continue to be a global epidemic that kills, torture, and maims-physically, psychologically, sexually and economically. It is one of the most pervasive of Human Rights Violations, denying women and girls equality, security, dignity, self-worth and human rights to enjoy fundamental freedoms. Violation against women is present in every country, cutting across boundaries of culture, class, education, income, ethnicity and age. Even though most societies proscribe violence against women, the realitiy is that violation against women's human rights are often sanctioned under the garb of cultural practices and norms or through misinterpretation of religious tenets. Sidney Brandon has rightly said that 'statistically it is safer to be on streets after dark with a stranger than at home in bosom of one's family, for it is there that account murder and violence are likely to occur' Therefore, no society can claim to be free of such violence. The only variation is in the pattern and trends that exist in control of the region.

The various problems touched upon in these articles are- criminalization of marital rape whereupon various court cases in Indian and foreign courts are reviewed and decisions of the apex courts are illustrated. Marital Rape exemption has granted husbands a right to have sexual intercourse with his wife though it is against her will and wishes or by making force against her. Marital Rape is preferably the worst type of rape, because it is some one a women knows, trusts, love, who commits this heinous act. Marital exemption and its historical background is delineated in the article. It further classifies the marital rape and its types. The study examines legal framework regarding marital exemption in India. The recommendations of the Law Commission were drafted in form of Indian Penal Cod. Various articles and provisions in the Indian Constitution are also examined like equal protection of law and equality before law, right to life, and personal liberty. Marital Rape is cruelty and is domestic violence and finally various reasons for making marital rape as an offence is argued in the article. Finally the study reviews the position of marital rape in other countries and various provisions and articles enshrined in the United Nations various conventions and covenants are also discussed like Convention on the elimination of discrimination against women (CEDAW).

The other problems related to the domestic violence against women are discussed which are-, Domestic Violence Act and its various articles and its pros and cons against man and women alike, salient features of the act are illustrated and explained- like it is a comprehensive enactment, right of women to secure housing, issuing of Protection Orders, appointment of Protection Officers, monetary benefits, penalties under the Act. For the understanding of laymen, various legal terms used in the Act are explained as Aggrieved Person, Domestic Relationship, Respondent, domestic Violations (legal understanding), Shared Household. By citing various cases decided by the apex court (Supreme Court), the role of the Judiciary in the problem of women in elaborately explained. It is also brought forth the cases concerning women against men, women are generally preferred. The author forwards various fruitful suggestions in the concluding part of the article.

Sexual Harassment met by the Indian Women, is also a rising problem in modern times in the BPO industry. BPO industry in India started in 1990. India is a unanimous choice across the globe to the availability of a large amount of cheap but skilled manpower. In India Information Technology-BPO industry, women are a key and vital part of our workforce. BPO is one of the fastest growing segments of the ITES industry. The article outline a complete picture of BPO industry across Indian States. After full explanation of BPO industry in India and women participation in workforce working in BPO industry, the study cites latest nasty incidents like murder of a few women working in BPO while going home back during night. Several security measures adopted by the BPO authorities for the safety of women in BPO Call Centres are also illustrated to avoid such nasty incidents in future.

The other articles included in the present volume are- Intimate Partner Violence, Honour Crimes, Domestic Violence against Women, Child Abuse, Domestic Violence Experienced by working and Nor-Working women in urban and rural areas of Jammu region, Violence against Kenyan's Women-some Issues, Ban on Burqa, Working Women: Problems, Statutes and Judicial decisions, Elder Abuse, Violence against women in India, Child Sexual Abuse-Snatching the Smile for Ever, Policies and framework to prevent Child Abuse in Street Children: An Indian Perspectives. There are plethora of problems seen and unseen enshrined in these articles which could encourage suggestive studies on them. These problems, as far as, possible are plainly discussed in this volume.

Article on CHILD ABUSE is a very learned and researched one touching national and international dimensions. Opens with Federal Child Abuse Prevention and Treatment Act (CAPTA) which defines child abuse very beautifully- ' The term "child abuse" and neglect means, at a minimum, any recent act or failure to act on the part of a parent or caretaker, which results in death, serious physical or emotional harm, sexual abuse or exploitation, or an act or failure to act which present an imminent risk of serious harm'.

Child abuse is a violation of the basic human rights of a child and is an outcome of a set of inter-related familial, social, psychological and economic factors. The problem of child abuse and human rights violation is one of the most criminal matters on the international human rights agenda. Child Abuse contributes to teen prostitution. More than 95% of teenage prostitute have been sexually abused. Teenage prostitution leads to drugs abuse and other serious crimes. Long term effects of child abuse are fear, anxiety, depression, anger, hostility, inappropriate sexual behaviour, poor self esteem, tendency towards substance abuse and difficulty with close relationships. The article enunciates major types of abuse, like emotional, neglect, physical, and sexual. It sorts out main reasons and causes of child abuse in our society. It also reviews government efforts to prevent abuse like home visitor program. Besides explaining its impacts on society, it suggests remedies to prevent the abuse.

One of the most important article is "Ban on Burqa" which is currently catching eye on account of security against spreading terrorism in the whole world. One of the strategy of terrorist is to employ women in the mission and smuggle arms or information to desired country. The legitimacy of burqa is a burning issue throughout the world especially after an absolute ban by France. The ban has been imposed due to many considerations like oppression of women, hindrance in development, discrimination issues, security reasons. Wearing of hijab or burqa is currently an issue in Singapore, Germany, Egypt, Russia, Italy, Holland, Turkey and may other countries. The paper briefly discusses provisions of burqa in the Holy Quran related to or alleged to be related to burqa, social consequences of burqa and legal consequences of burqa etc. The various heads of discussion in the article are-Burqa in Islam, International Obligations like CEDAW Conventions, does burqa violates rights of women-arguments in favour and against are stated, should India follow France? India is a party to various international treaties, conventions/covenants, like CEDAW, ICCPR, ICESCR, UDHR, which impose a duty on the state to protect a major population from gradual deterioration. Portion of the article is devoted to the fact that whether India should Ban Burqa- after the discussion, it is stated that it is not possible to ban burqa in India. However, there are obligations on India similar to France, to take all measures to eliminate violence or discrimination against women.

MS Benjamin in his article "Working Women - Problems, Statutes and Judicial Decisions" brings to light the real problems faced by women in the workplace and how the judiciary treats to solve such problems using the provisions enshrined in the constitution of India, statutes and international conventions and treaties as an instrument of ensuring equality and safety of women. Various provisions in the Constitution of India and other enactments have been cited by the author. Various judicial decisions given by the apex court have been cited. In addition to constitutional provisions, court cases, ILO Regulations, the author discusses sexual harassment at working places. Until 1980, no attempt has been made to evolve any measure to counter the problem of sexual harassment of women in general and women workers in particular. For the first time, United States in 1980, set up the American Equal Employment Opportunity Commission (EEOC), along with a set of guidelines dealing with sexual harassment. In UK, the courts have held sexual harassment to be a conduct prohibited by the sexual discrimination act, 1975. Judiciary has gone pro-women in such cases where women are posed against men.

Readers/research scholars and students of sociology will themselves observe that all the eighteen articles which are specifically devoted to domestic violence contain fabulous information like various statistics, international covenants/conventions, constitutions of various countries, landmark court cases by apex court of concerned country, current substance matter on the related subject which can be consulted and quoted. Articles on domestic violence against women collected and collated at one place prove to be valuable publication. The book can also form a part of side reference book for consultation on the said topics on national and international level.

CRIMINALIZATION OF MARITAL RAPE: AN ANALYSIS

*Rattan Singh** *& Jasdeep Kaur***

Women have always been perceived as the weaker class. They have been subjugated for ages. They have been victim of many atrocities and crime. The situation still remains the same though the common perception is that women have been emancipated. Perhaps their emancipation is true to some extent. However much still needs to be done. Till now the focus has been on eradicating the violence against women which occurs outside the home that is the crime by strangers. Yet perhaps the cruelest crime a women is subjected to is, to face carnage at the hands of those she trusts and loves. There are numerous enactments and legislations passed regarding violence against the women in her own house like dowry, domestic violence and cruelty. However the biggest, the most shameful and degrading wrong has failed to gain any recognition as a crime in the eyes of all the policy makers. The crime of where a husband forces himself upon his wife, the crime of where a man thinks that it is his nuptial right to have sex with his wife, namely Marital Rape.[1]

Justice Oliver Wendall Holmes once wrote: "It is revolting to have no better reason for a rule of law than that so it was laid down in the time of Henry IV. It is still more revolting if the grounds upon which it was laid down have vanished long since, and the rule simply persists from a blind imitation of the past."[2] In a country like India, which distinguishes itself in the practice of inheriting colonial legacies, no other law captures the spirit of Justice Holmes statement in a better way than the doctrine of Marital Exemption to the rape law in India. Marital rape as an exemption is a product of English Common Law as

* *Reader, Department of Laws, Guru Nanak Dev University, Amritsar, (Punjab).*

** *Lecturer in Law, Rayat and Bahra College of Law, Sahauran, Mohali, (Punjab).*

the Indian penal Code was enacted by the then English authorities.[3] Marital Rape exemption has granted husband a right to have sexual intercourse with his wife though it is against her wishes, or by making use of force against her. Thus Marital Rape is any unwanted sexual act by the spouse committed without the consent or against a person's will obtain by force or threat of force.

Marital Rape is preferably the worst kind of rape, because it is someone a woman knows, trust and love, who commits this heinous act. Women who are raped by their husbands are raped and likely to be raped many times. They experience not only vaginal but also anal and oral rape. Husbands often rape their wives when they are asleep, or use coercion, threats, physical violence or weapons to force their wives to have sex with them. It is a serious kind of problem which most of the women in country suffers. It is difficult to obtain data on rape and violence with in the family, because victims are reluctant to report incidences as they may be hesitant to report because of family loyalty, fear of their abuser's contribution, inability to leave the relationship or like.[4] Rape is not merely a physical assault; it is often destructive of the whole personality of the victim. A murderer destroys the physical body of his victim; a rapist degrades the very soul of the helpless women.[5]

Historical Background of Marital Exemption

Throughout the history of most societies, it has been acceptable for men to force their wives to have sex with them against their will. The traditional definition of rape in most countries was sexual intercourse with a female not his wife without her consent." This provided husbands with an exemption from prosecution for raping their wives, a license to rape. The foundation of this exemption can be traced back to statement made by Sir Mathew Hale, in England in 17th century. Lord Hale wrote that the husband can not be guilty of a rape committed by himself upon his lawful wife, for their mutual matrimonial consent and the contract wife hath given herself up in this kind un to her husband which she can not retract.[6] As long as in 1869, John Stuart Mill observed that marital rape is never welcome to women for it represents surrender a dignity so complete that it makes the lot of women lower than the slave.[7] He is of the opinion that a female slave has an admitted right and is considered under the moral obligation to refuse her master last familiarity. Not so a wife, however brutal a tyrant she may, unfortunately be chained to, he can claim from her and enforce the lowest degradation of a human being, that of being made the instrument of an animal function contrary to her inclinations. Other than the theory of implied consent, there were two more doctrines that were the foundation of the marital exemption. The first was that rape was originally a property crime rather than a crime against the person. Under the ancient code rape was not a crime against a woman but a violation of the property rights of her father, brother or husband by the rapist. The women were considered as a piece of property to which damage has been caused. The punishment was therefore was for the damaged property that is, the rapist has to pay compensation to the women or marry her.[8] Another doctrine which is pleaded in favour of the marital exemption is that it is physically impossible to commit rape with in marriage because a man could not rape himself as the institution of marriage is itself based on the presumption that husband and wife are treated as one after their marriage. Moreover after marriage the wife is considered as having given irrevocable consent to sexual intercourse to the husband on marriage and hence the husband can not be guilty of committing rape on his wife.

Types of Marital Rape

It appears that Sexual violence is most likely to occur along with all other forms of violence like physical violence, emotional violence and economic violence. In fact, Violence can not be compartmentalized. It is a continum. Finkelhor & Yllo have tried to categorize the sexual assault into three major forms.

Battering Rapes: In this kind of rape women experience both physical and sexual violence in the relationship. Women who are raped and battered by their partners experience the violence in various ways - e.g. some are battered during the sexual violence or the rape may follow a physically violent episode where the husband wants to 'make up' and coerces his wife to have sex against her will.

Obsessive Rape: Other women experience could be labeled as 'sadistic' or 'obsessive' rape; these assaults involve torture and perverse sexual acts and are often physically violent. Pornography is frequently involved with sadistic forms of rape. The assaults are typically after the woman has refused sexual intercourse.

Force-only rape: In what is called *"force-only"* rape, husbands use only the amount of force necessary to coerce their wives; battering may not be characteristic of these relationships. The assaults are typically after the woman has refused sexual intercourse.

Legal Framework Regarding Marital Exemption in India

In India, marital rape is not recognized under the current legal definitions of rape. Section 375 of Indian Penal Code states that Sexual intercourse by a man with his own wife, the wife being under 15 years of age, is not rape. The code like the most penal codes incorporates a definition of rape evolved almost entirely on the basis of common Law. A nominal punishment under Section 376 (1) is provided if the wife is between 12 to 15 years of age or is living under a decree of judicial separation.[9] Apart from these two provisions, no provision is made for the married women's protection under the code. The law regarding marital rape has remained more o less unchanged since the introduction of Indian Penal Code. Till 1983, the law of marital rape has been amended thrice, however only change which was made in this provision was that of increase in the age of wife mentioned in the exception.[10] Even after 1983, no amendment has been made in the law relating to the marital exemption in India. Law Commission[11] in its recommendation had taken a step forward in reforming the Law relating to Marital Exemption. In its report, the commission had recommended two major changes. They were:

(i) The Law Commission recommended that marital rape should be removed from the scope of Section 375 and intercourse by a man in his minor wife should be placed in some other Section as a separate offence.

(ii) The Commission has also considered the position of legally separated wife and offence of rape. The Commission observed that:

"Under the exception, a husband can not be guilty of raping his wife if she is above the age of 15 years. This exception is to take note of one special situation, namely when the husband and wife are living apart under a decree of judicial separation or by a mutual consent. In this case, the marriage technically subsists and if the husband has sexual intercourse with her against her will with or without her consent, he will not be charged with the offence of rape. This does not appear to be right. We consider that in such case, sexual intercourse by a man with his wife without her consent will be punishable as offence."[12]

The recommendation of the Law Commission was drafted in the form of Indian Penal Code (Amendment Bill) 1972. However the recommendation remain unamended as the dissolution of the then Lok Sabha took place. These recommendations were again reviewed by Law Commission in 1980.[13] The Law commission considered that the age of the wife falling with in the exemption of marital rape should be extended to 18 years and sexual intercourse with a judicially separated wife should be made an offence. Accordingly on the basis of these recommendations, Criminal Law Amendment Act, 1983 was passed by the legislature incorporating these two provisions in the Law of marital rape. This was a welcome step. However much is needed to be done in this area of marital exemption.

Since then no change has been made in the exemption relating to marital rape. The successive Law Commissions have stopped to recognize marital rape on the same footing as that of the non marital offence of rape. The opportunity was again given to the Law Commission to express its opinion upon this matter; however, the commission had missed a golden opportunity.[14]

Under an order in 1999 made while considering Writ Petition of 1997[15], the Supreme Court of India requested the Law Commission "to examine the issues raised by the petitioners and examine the feasibility of making recommendations for amendment of the Indian Penal Code or deal with the same in any other manner so as to plug the loopholes. The petitioner `Sakshi', an organization interested in the issues concerning women, had approached the Supreme Court of India with the aforesaid Writ Petition praying for (a) issuance of a writ in the nature of a declaration or any other appropriate writ or direction declaring inter alia that 'sexual intercourse' as contained in section 375 of the Indian Penal Code shall be amended and the exception to this Section should be deleted. The Law Commission was not made a party to the Writ Petition. The Supreme Court however directed the Law Commission, to indicate its response with respect to the issues raised in the said Writ Petition. The Law Commission[16] gave its recommendation on this provision and disagrees with the opinion expressed by the organization for the deletion of the exception.

The Commission was of the view that where a husband causes some physical injury to his wife, he is punishable under the appropriate offence and the fact that he is the husband of the victim is not an extenuating circumstance recognized by law; if so, there is no reason why concession should be made in the matter of offence of rape/sexual assault where the wife happens to be above 15/16 years. The Commission was not satisfied with the suggestion that this Exception should be recommended to be deleted since that may amount to excessive interference with the marital relationship.

Constitutional Perspective of Marital Rape Exemption

The Constitution of India is the grund norm from which other Laws are extracted. Each law that is passed in this country has to be in conformity with the principles and the ideas enshrined in the Constitution. Every Law that is passed in the country should confirm to the principles and ideas laid down in the Constitution. Any law which fails to meet this standard is liable to struck down as unconstitutional. It is submitted that the Law relating to marital exemption violates and is not in conformity with the principles enshrined in Art. 14 and 21 of the Constitution.

Equal Protection of Law and Equality before Law[17]

Article 14 of the Constitution provides that the state shall not deny any person equality before Law or equal protection of Law with in its territory. It does not mean that absolute equality among the human beings. It is a concept implying absence of any special privilege by reason of birth, creed or like in favour of the individual and also the equal subject of all the individuals and classes to ordinary Law of land. The equal protection clause means that reasonable classification is permitted but not class legislation.[18] Class Legislation is which makes improper discrimination by conferring privileges upon a class of persons arbitrary selected from a large number of persons.[19] Classification to be reasonable has to fulfil two conditions[20]:

(i) The Classification must be founded on an intelligible differntia which distinguish the persons or things that are grouped together from others left out of the group:

(ii) The differentia must have a rational relation to the object sought to be achieved by the Act.

It is submitted that the exemption given to marital rape does not satisfy both the criteria laid down in different cases and also not according to the valid classification as laid down by the Constitution itself. Section 375 of Indian Penal Code makes a classification in terms of the exemption that does not regard forceful sexual intercourse in a marriage as rape.

Right to Life and Personal Liberty[21]

Article 21 of the Constitution provides that no person shall be deprived of his life or personal liberty except according to procedure established by Law. Prior to Maneka Gandhi's decision, Article 21 guaranteed the right to life and personal liberty to citizens only against the arbitrary action of the executive and not from legislative action.[22] But after Maneka Gandhi's decision Article 21 now protects the right of life and personal liberty not only from executive but from legislative action also.[23] In this case the Court gave a new dimension to Article 21. It was held that the right to live is not merely confined to physical existence but it includes with in its ambit the right to live with human dignity. It also includes with in scope the Right to Health as is decided in different cases from time to time.[24] In another case the court held that women also have the right to life and liberty, they also have the right to be respected and treated as equal citizens. Their honour and dignity can not be touched or violated. They also have the right to lead an honourable and peaceful life.[25]

If we make an analysis of this particular Article of the Constitution, then it may be found that the marital exemption clause violates Article 21 of the Constitution as it is against the principle of living in human dignity, honour of the wife concerned as in certain circumstances when she is forced to have sexual intercourse against her will. This situation has relevance in the Observation of Justice Saghir Ahmed, he observed that "Unfortunately, a women in our country, belongs to a class for group of society who are in disadvantageous position on the account of several social barriers and impediments and have therefore, been victim of tyranny at the hands of men with whom they unfortunately enjoy equal status under the Constitution."[26]

Marital Rape as Cruelty

It will be useful to point out that Section 498 A of Indian Penal Code, 1860 amply covers the cause of victims of marital rape since marital rape is a form of cruelty which is perpetrated by the husband on his wife. The explanation to this Section provides that willful conduct which is of such a nature as is likely to cause danger to health, whether physical or mental of the women accords ample flexibility to cover the cause of a victim of marital rape. It is, however submitted that in spite of the fact that an offender of marital rape can be punished under this Section, the fall out of doing so would amount to comprising on realization of reality that rape does happen with in private sphere of marriage. Reading rape in to Section 498 A would amount to still recognizing the fact of husband being the rapist as a mitigating circumstances since the punishment accorded for cruelty under Section 498 A is imprisonment up to 3 years and fine as opposed to the punishment of imprisonment not less than 7 years, which may extend to life or 10 years and fine.[27] Therefore, it is important to grant legal recognition to marital rape as rape since rape is rape irrespective of who commits.[28]

Marital Rape as Domestic Violence

One significant step was taken for the protection of women from all kind of violence against her in the shape of Protection of Women from Domestic Violence Act, 2005. The Act covers all the aspect of domestic violence like physical, emotional, sexual and economic abuses. It affects security, equality, dignity, health and even life of women guaranteed by various human rights instruments.[29] Although the Act is comprehensive in its categorization of domestic violence, which represents a departure from previous, narrower characterizations of domestic violence, it is clearly inadequate to deal with the problem of marital rape. The problem of marital rape goes much beyond the issue of domestic violence and the Act does not deal with it. Marital rape is a unique problem that encompasses both physical and psychological trauma of being raped by someone who has taken marriage vows to love and honour her spouse.[30] Although the words marital rape is not used in this particular Act, however indirectly it involves the issue of marital rape. But the tragedy is that it is just made as a civil offence which is not sufficient.

Reasons for Making Marital Rape as an Offence

There are many people who are against the Criminalization of Marital Rape. Different type of reasoning is given by different persons for not deleting the exemption clause from the sphere of Indian Penal Code.

Social Issue Rather than Legal: Marital rape is considered as a social issue rather than legal issue in India. India is a male dominated society and husband is considered 'Pati Parmeshwar.' The view point in India is that with marriage comes fulfilling husband's conjugal rights and wife can not refuse him. So even if she is raped by her husband, she finds it difficult to come out with it. Various subliminal messages across the media and through society encourage young boys to believe in the sexual availability of women. Men begin to believe that decision making progress is their sole prerogative, that their wives do not have any rights in those matters that their wives are subject to them in every respect. Even educated persons, who would otherwise treat women with great respect, would thing nothing of having sex with their wives, against their wives wishes.[31] However if this type of thinking is being followed then other offences which violates the rights of women can never get recognition which violates the social regime at that particular period of time when they were made part of Law like Prevention of Sati System, Dowry Prohibition, Indecent representation of Women etc.

Individual Rights Approach to Marital Rape: Those who defend marital rape exemption rely on cultural assumptions about men, women and the marital relationship. These assumptions ignore the individual rights of women with in marriage. Supporters of marital exemption argue that it protects the privacy of married couple and it promotes marital harmony and reconciliation. The assumption is that no injury can come from the marriage, since husband and the wife are always in agreement, leads to the view that legal intervention in the form of the complete criminalization of marital rape would be an unwanted introduction of an antagonism in to marriage.[32] However, the people who are thinking in this way have forgot that there is concept of equality which is provided to the citizens of India among which women are also included, then how a Law based on inequality can survive relating to individual rights of women.

Difficulty in Enforcement of the Provision: One of the arguments that come up against the criminalization of marital rape is the difficulty encountered in its enforcement. People propound that there is a line that has to be drawn between private life and public life and that the executive and Judiciary can not enter the four walls of a domestic household. There is nothing like interfering in the private sphere of the individual with the deletion of the exemption clause as more than interference, it is a threat to the freedom, liberty, life and dignity of the women as she continues to live with that person who is the real predator in her life.

Problem with Evidence and Fabricating False Claim: Another justification to continue the exemption clause is that it may lead to false charges being leveled against the husband. The problem is not limited to this clause only. Any kind of Law can be violated in this way by framing false evidence. Only on this very assumption the exemption clause can not be retained as it is more stigmatic to women than this problem of false evidence. Moreover, the provision is already there that deals with fabricating false evidence.[33] If need be amendment can further be made in this Section.

Marital Rape as Uncommon Offence: Some people argue that as the offence of marital rape is uncommon, so there is no need to make an amendment in Law relating to it. But the real Position is not so. It is just that is it mostly unreported crime in India due to a number of reasons which include societal set up, fear of being ridiculed, no knowledge about the offence being committed. Minimal cases which are reported reflect the serious nature of the offence committed against wife.

Permanent Consent as a Rationale: It is seen from the provision of Section 375 of Indian Penal Code that consent is the fundamental issue. This is very crucial and requires that the sexual activity should be without the consent of the woman. Te institution of marriage as regards the patriarchal society is based on the consent which is given in relation to sexual intercourse with a wife also and treated as itself implicit in it and she can not refuse to have sexual intercourse.

Thus if it is satisfied that the women failed to resist, then it termed as consent given in a particular case even under ordinary rape. But one should see the plea of the wife who has been sexually victimized that she may not be able to muster enough strength to repel the act. She can be in the sate of shock and fear. A woman is not normally expected to assault a man because of her physique and placement in the society. Many a times she is rendered helpless to do anything. So this rationale has no application so far as the exemption of marital rape is concerned.[34]

Position of Marital Rape in Other Countries

For the past three decades there has been massive legislative and judicial activity around the world with regard to law of Marital Rape. Years of extensive scrutiny, sustained criticism, and persistent activity have resulted in a significant, positive and at least arguably, far reaching steps to abolish this exemption. In England, House of Lords in R v. R[35] announced that husband's immunity as expounded by Hale no longer exists. It was followed by the amendment Act of 1994, which formally abolish the exemption in England.[36] In 1993, marital rape has become a crime in all the state of United Nations, under at least one or other Section of the Sexual Offences Code. The Marital Rape exemption was abolished in New Zealand in the year 1985 when Section 128 to Crimes Act, 1961 was enacted. The Act provides that a person can be convicted of sexual violence in respect of sexual connection with another person notwithstanding that they are married at the time the sexual connection occurred.[37] Canadian Law has also made it as an offence. According to Canadian Criminal Code, marital Rape is a crime against women.[38]

Marital Rape is also considered as a crime under International Law according to the UN General Assembly. Marital Rape was specifically mentioned in Beijing Declaration and Platform for action. The convention on Elimination of Discrimination against Women (CEDAW), adopted in 1979 by UN Assembly, is often described as an international bill of rights for women. Consisting of Preamble and articles, it defines what constitutes discrimination against women and sets up an agenda for national action to end such discrimination. The convention describes discrimination against women as:

> "Any discrimination, exclusion or restriction made on the basis of sex which has the effect or purpose of impairing or nullifying the recognition, enjoyment or exercise by women irrespective of their marital status, on basis of equality of men and women, human rights and fundamental freedoms in the political, economic, social, cultural, civil or any other field."

As the legal status of women has changed the concept of a married men's marital right to sexual intercourse has become less widely held. In December 1993, the United Nations High Commissioner for Human Rights published the Declaration on Elimination of Violence against Women. This established marital rape as a human right violation.[39]

Conclusion

Marriage in modern times is regarded as a partnership of equals and is no longer in consonance with the idea as per which a wife was considered as a chattel of the husband. Rape is Rape no matter who commits it and the fact that the rapist happens to be the husband of the victim does not and can not give rise to the notion that a husband can not be guilty of raping a wife. By exempting marital rape, law through the medium of the Indian Penal Code, 1860 is in a way forcing upon an unwilling party a positive act of sex. As has rightly been stated "nothing can be more degrading to human dignity and monstrous to human spirit than to subject a person by the long arm of law to a positive sexual act."[40] The more depressing fact is that the victim of marital rape will have to face such behaviour in future also and be constantly reminded of her violation by her husband.

Moreover the state by providing for such exemption is discriminating between victims of rape by a stranger and victim of rape by husband. A woman may be clear in her mind that she does not want to have sex with the man she knows. In such situations involving two persons who are familiar with one another, it is not necessary that she should resist violently so as to make him understand that she does not want sex. The Law must recognize that a husband can rape his wife and marriage does not give him the right to have sexual intercourse with his wife against her wishes.[41]

The law which distinguishes between the age of wife relating to the exemption of marital rape, by no means to be followed as giving absolute authority to husband to have control over her. That of course can not be supposed. Under no system of Law in this country whether Hindu or Mohammedan or that framed under the British Law, has it ever been the Law. If the Law is such then it is certain death to her or that it is probably dangerous to her life.[42]

Marital Rape has been considered to be not an offence since ages, but the time has come that we as a nation start thinking like a reasonable and responsible nation. Married women are supposed to be a symbol of purity and should be respected. Perhaps the offence of Marital rape is more of a crime than other crimes as along with shame and violation that accompanied other rapes, marital rape is accompanied with a feeling of betrayal and a sense of loss. Women need to break this cycle that they are caught in. Men had to realize that robbing their wives of their glory is not the way to show women who the Lord of the house is.

Notes

1. Kritika Venugopal, "Criminalisation of Marital Rape," *Criminal Law Journal*, December 2006, p. 306.
2. Oliver W. Holmes, *"The Path of Law,"* Vol. 10 Harvard Law Review, 1897, p. 457 & 469.

3. See Draft Code of the Indian Penal Code which was prepared and completed in 1850 and was Presented to Legislative Assembly in 1856 and was Passed in to Law in 1860 by the Act XLV.
4. Subansh Chandra Singh, "Marital Rape: How Offensive is it?" *Criminal Law Journal,* July 2009, p. 194.
5. State of Punjab v. Gurmit Singh (1996) 2 SCC 384.
6. Mathew Hale, *History of the Pleas of the Crown,* Vol. I, 1736, p. 629.
7. J. S. Mill, "The Subjection of Women," S. M. Okin, Indianapolis, 1988, p. 33.
8. Manu Smriti, p. 366.
9. See Section 375, Exception, of Indian Penal Code, 1860 and Section 376 A of Indian penal Code, 1860.
10. See Amendment Act 10 of 1891, 29 of1925 and 42 of 1949 of Indian Penal Code, 1860.
11. The Law Commission of India, 42nd Report on Indian Penal Code, June 1971.
12. The Law Commission of India, 42nd Report on Indian Penal Code, June 1971, Para 16, p. 115.
13. The Law Commission of India, 84th Report on Rape and Allied offences: Some Questions of Substantive Law, Procedure and Evidence, 1980.
14. The Law Commission of India, 172nd Report on Review of Rape Laws, March 2000.
15. Sakshi v. Union of India AIR 2004 SC 3566.
16. The Law Commission of India, 172nd Report on Review of Rape Laws, March 2000.
17. See Article 14 of Constitution of India, 1950.
18. Jagjit Singh v. State AIR 1954 Hyd 28.
19. R. K. Garg v. Union of India AIR 1980 SC 2138.
20. K. Thimmappa v. Chairman Central Board of Directors SBI, AIR 2001 SC 467.
21. See Section 21 of Constitution of India, 1950.
22. A. K. Gopolan v. State of Madras AIR 1950 SC 27.
23. Manek Gandhi v. Union of India AIR 1978 SC 597.
24. Parmanand Katara v. Union of India AIR 1989 SC 2039, Consumer Education and Research Centre v. Union of India (1995) 3 SCC 42.
25. Bodhisathwa Gautam v. Subhra Chakraborty (1996) 1 SCC 490.
26. *Ibid.*
27. See Section 376 of Indian Penal Code, 1860.
28. Vasundra Goel, Role of Judiciary in untying the Knot: Judicial Process and Unconstitutionality of the Marital Rape Exemption under IPC, *Criminal Law Journal,* November 2007, p. 239.
29. See Section 3 of Protection of Women from Domestic Violence Act, 2005.
30. Morgan Lee Wolley, "Marital Rape: A Unique Blend of Domestic Violence and Non Marital Rape," *Hasting Women Law Journal,* Vol. 8, p. 269.
31. Rakesh Kr. Singh, "Trauma of Marital Rape: Husband Turns Predator," *Criminal Law Journal,* April 2008, p. 103.

32. Subhash Chandra, *Ibid* Note 4, p. 202.
33. See Section Chapter XI "Of False Evidence and Offences against Public Justice," Indian penal Code, 1860.
34. Lina Gonsalves, "Rape: Some reflections on the Need to Amend the Existing Law," *Criminal Law Journal*, 205, p. 245.
35. (1991) 2 ALL ER 747.
36. See Section 147 of Sexual Offences Act, 1994.
37. See 128 (4) of Crimes Act, 1961.
38. See 246 (8) of Canadian Code Which Abolish Marital Rape Exemption through Criminal Law Amendment Act, 1990.
39. *Ibid.*, Note 4, p. 200.
40. Bohisattwa Gautam v. Subhra Chakraborty (1996) 1SCC 490, P. 366.
41. *Ibid.*, Note 34, p. 246.
42. Queen Empress v. Huree Mohun Mythee (1890) 18 Original Criminal Cases, Cal 49.

DOMESTIC VIOLENCE ACT: A MILE STONE OF PROTECTION

*Arvindeka Chaudhary**

Statistically it is safer to be on streets after dark with a stranger than at home in bosom of one's family, for it is there that accident, murder and violence are likely to occur.
SIDNEY BRANDON

Introduction

Violence against women and girls continues to be a global epidemic that kills, tortures and maims-physically, psychologically, sexually and economically. It is one of the most pervasive of human rights violations, denying women and girls equality, security, dignity, self-worth and their right to enjoy fundamental freedoms.

Violence against women is present in every country, cutting across boundaries of culture, class, education, income, ethnicity and age. Even though most societies proscribe violence against women, the reality is that violations against women's human rights are often sanctioned under the garb of cultural practices and norms, or through misinterpretation of religious tenets. Moreover, when the violation takes place within the home, as is very often the case, the abuse is effectively condoned by the tacit silence and the passivity displayed by the State and the law-enforcing machinery. No society can claim to be free of such violence; the only variation is in the patterns and trends that exist in countries and regions.[1]

The term domestic violence implies the incidents of familiar or intimate battering having reference to an idealised family unit functioning in a protected and secluded manner, appropriately shielded from the public.[2] Familiarity with the perpetrator and filial values deter resistance, "closed doors"

* *Phd. Student, Department of Laws, Guru Nanak Dev University, Amritsar, (Punjab).*

alienate the victim from the remedies, resulting in a convenient status quo where the victim reconciles and the society can connive. Domestic violence explodes the myth that women are subjected to harassment and violence on the streets and at their workplaces while the home is the safest "haven".[3]

History of Domestic Violence

Domestic violence is as old as recorded history. It has been reported in virtually every society in every country since the dawn of time. Throughout the course of history domestic violence has been both legal and socially acceptable until very recently[4]. Physical force has always been used to keep subordinate groups in their place by the more dominant forces in the society. Most societies have been male dominated. Historically, women have been oppressed and beaten with the approval of societies dominated by men.

The earliest known civilization appeared in the near East between 4000 and 3000 B.C.E. in Egypt and Mesopotamia. It was remarkable that Egyptian allowed women to succeed throne but recent evidence has emerged suggesting that domestic violence was not uncommon even then. In 1977, Paleopathologists revealed that female Egyptian mummies had more skull fractures than male mummies even though men were warriors of the society. It has been hypothesized that these fractures were inflicted on women during domestic disputes.

The first known written law Hammurabi's Code represented an important advancement that all men are equal but even under Code men had the ultimate control and power. The code included jumping in the river for her husband if a wife was accused of adultery or becoming a slave in her husband's home if she neglected the husband or plunged him into debt and being cast into the water for not being congenial to her husband.

In the Roman Empire a woman could be stoned to death if her husband accused her of not being a virgin on their wedding night. Woman was treated as a property and her husband as an aggrieved by the damaged goods of a non-virginal wife.

By 1740 violence in the home became a "private" moral crime instead of a social concern and the curtains of the home closed on violence within. In the early 1800 a wave of reform movements sweep the United States. A notable opponent of domestic violence was the Women's Temperance Movement who focused on the effect of alcoholism on the family unit. But in 1824 the Supreme Court of Mississippi held that a man is allowed to chastise his wife without being subject to vexatious prosecution because that would only bring shame on all the parties involved.

In 1835 the Temperance Reformers kicked the high gear when first drawing ever in the United States was printed and by 1840, the domestic violence achieved the legitimacy of being "newsworthy". In 1848 a growth of new ideas on women's rights produced a new political activism within the Temperance Reform Movement. The Seneca Falls Convention convened to propose rights for women. The Declaration oh Human Sentiment identified a series of women's grievances against the male tyranny.

Domestic violence cut across every segment of society and occurs in all age, racial, ethnic, socio-economic, sexual orientation and religious groups. Domestic violence is a social, economic and health concern that does not discriminate.[5] It is one of the big issues of present times particularly in a country like India which is male-dominated and where the physical abuse of women in their homes is rampant.

Constitutional Perspectives: Protection of Women and Fundamental Rights

Before the commencement of this Act, Supreme Court has played a very important role in interpreting and giving a new shape to feministic administration of justice to the indian womenhood. While delivering its bold judgments the Supreme Court upheld the dignity of women by holding the right to live with dignity and violence free society. Some of the following observations are worth mentioning:

The Right to be Free of Violence

In *Francis Coralie Mullin v.Administrator, Union Territory Delhi,*[6] the Supreme Court stated, any act which damages or injures or interferes with the use of any limb or faculty of a person, either permanently or even temporarily, would be within the inhibition of Article 21. This right is incorporated in the Act through the definition of physical abuse, which constitutes domestic violence (and is hence punishable under the Act). Physical abuse is said to consist of acts or conduct of such nature that they cause bodily pain, harm, or danger to life, limb or health, or impair the health or development of the aggrieved person. Apart from this, the Act also includes similar acts of physical violence and certain acts of physical violence as envisaged in the Indian Penal Code within the definition of domestic violence. By adoption of such an expansive definition, the Act protects the right of women against violence.

The Right to live with Dignity

In *Ahmadabad Municipal Corporation v. Nawab Khan Gulab Khan*[7], the Supreme Court emphasized the fact that the right to life included in its ambit the right to live with human dignity, basing its opinion on a host of cases that had been decided in favour of this proposition. The right to dignity would include the right against being subjected to humiliating sexual acts. It would also include the right against being insulted. These two facets of the right to life find mention under the definitions of sexual abuse and emotional abuse, respectively. A praiseworthy aspect of the legislation is the very conception of emotional abuse as a form of domestic violence. The recognition of sexual abuse of the wife by the husband as a form of violation to the person is creditable, especially as such sexual abuse is not recognised by the IPC as an offence. These acts would fall within the confines of domestic violence as envisaged by the Act, though the definition would not be limited to it.

The Right to Shelter

In *Chameli Singh v. State of U.P.*[8], it was held that the right to life would include the right to shelter. Ss. 6 and 17 of the Domestic Violence Act reinforce this right. Under S.6, it is a duty of the Protection Officer to provide the aggrieved party accommodation where the party has no place of accommodation, on request by such party or otherwise. Under S.17, the party's right to continue staying in the shared household is protected. These provisions thereby enable women to use the various protections given to them without any fear of being left homeless.[9]

The Protection of Women from Domestic Violence Act, 2005

The phenomenon of domestic violence has been widely prevalent but remained largely ignored in the legal domain. Acting on the lines and responding to the voices which were raised by women's organisations, the Domestic Violence Act, 2005 was passed recognising violence between the four walls of the house. The Act was passed by the Parliament with recourse to Article 253 of the Constitution. This provision confers on the Parliament the power to make laws in pursuance of international treaties, conventions, etc. The Domestic Violence Act was passed in furtherance of the recommendations of the United Nations Committee on the Convention on Elimination of All Forms of Discrimination Against Women (CEDAW). The Act encompasses all the provisions of the Specific Recommendations which form a part of General Recommendation no. 19, 1992.

Domestic Violence Act 2005 is the first significant attempt in India to recognise domestic abuse as a punishable offence, to extend its provisions to those in live-in relationships. The Act covers not just the wife but any woman who is the sexual partner of the male irrespective of whether she is his legal wife or not. In fact, any woman residing in the household who is related in some way to the respondent is covered by the Act. The information regarding an act or acts of domestic violence does not necessarily have to be lodged by the aggrieved party but the same can be done by "any person who has reason to believe that" such an act has been or is being committed as a consequence neighbors, relatives, social workers can all take necessary steps to help the victim[10] and all crimes in the Domestic Violence Act are non-bailable. For the first time, the law has expanded the definition to include sexual, verbal and economic violence. The new law is also tough on men who subject women to name calling or verbal abuse. Another significant step is to recognize economic violence which includes not providing money, food, clothes, medicines or causing hindrance to employment opportunities.

The Act provides for a better and effective protection to women of rights which the Constitution of India guarantees to them and from violence occurring within the family or any other matter which is connected therewith or is incidental thereto.

Salient Features of the Act

Comprehensive Enactment

This Act covers all those women who are or have been in a relationship with the abuser where both parties have lived together in a shared household and are related by consanguinity, marriage or through a relationship in the nature of the marriage or adoption. In addition, relationship with family members living together as a joint family is also covered under the Act. Even those women who are sisters, widows, mothers or single woman living with the abuser are entitled to legal protection under the present enactment. Children are also covered by the Act; they too can file a case against a parent or parents who are torturing them either physically, mentally, or economically. Any person can file a complaint on behalf of a child. As defined under Section 2(b) of the Act the expression child includes any adopted, step or foster child.

Right of Women to Secure Housing

It provides for the right of woman to reside in her matrimonial home or shared household irrespective of the fact whether she has any right or title in such home or household. This right is secured by residence order which is passed by the magistrate. Also, the magistrate may direct the respondent to remove himself from shared household or restrain him or his relatives from entering in the shared household and not to alienate or dispose off the shared household.

Magistrate to Issue Protection Order

The Act empowers the magistrate to pass protection order, after giving the aggrieved person and respondent an opportunity of being heard, in favour of the aggrieved person to prevent respondent from aiding or abetting or committing any act of domestic violence to the aggrieved or her relatives or any other who provides her assistance from domestic violence. The protection order may prohibit the respondent to visit workplace or school if the aggrieved is child or any place frequented by the aggrieved. The respondent also cannot alienate any assets or operate bank lockers or bank accounts belonging to them jointly or separately to respondent or any other property which may cause violence to dependents. The Respondent cannot during the pending disposal of the case prohibit or restrict the aggrieved continued access to resources or facilities to which she is entitled by virtue of the domestic relationship, including access to the shared household.

Appointment of Protection Officers

It provides for appointment of Protection Officers[11] and registration of non-governmental organisations as service providers for providing assistance to the aggrieved person with respect to her medical examination, obtaining legal aid, safe shelter, etc.[12]

Monetary Relief

The Act empowers the magistrate to pass monetary relief to aggrieved from the respondent to meet the expenses and loss suffered which includes loss of earning, loss to property and medical expenses and maintenance of the aggrieved and her children in addition to Sec.125 of the Code of the Criminal Procedure, 1973 or any other law for the time being in force.[13] The amount of maintenance may be paid in lump some or monthly payments. Further, it provides that monetary relief shall be adequate, reasonable and consistence with the living standard of the aggrieved.[14]

Penalties Under the Act

It provides that a breach of protection order or an interim protection order shall be an offence for which respondent may be awarded imprisonment which may extend for one year or fine upto twenty thousand rupees or with both.[15] Also, the magistrate is empowered to frame charges under Sec.498-A or any other relevant provision or provisions of Indian Penal Code 1860 or the Dowry Prohibition Act, 1961 if facts disclose commission of any offence under these Acts.[16]

Important Expressions Used Under the Act

Aggrieved Person

According to Sec. 2(a) of the Act, expression "aggrieved person" means any woman who is or has been in a domestic relationship with the 'respondent' and who alleges to have been subjected to any act of domestic violence by the respondent.[17]

Domestic Relationship

Section 2(c) defines "domestic relationship" as a relationship between two persons who live or have, at any time, lived together in a shared household when they are related by consanguinity, marriage or through a relationship in the nature of marriage, adoption or are family members living together as a joint family.[18]

Respondent

Section 2 (q) states that any adult male member who has been in a domestic relationship with the aggrieved person is the 'respondent'. The respondent can also be a relative of the husband or male partner. Thus, a father-in-law, mother-in-law, or even siblings of the husband and other relatives can be proceeded against.

Domestic Violence

The Act, in a bold break from prior legislations, gives a very expansive definition to the term "domestic violence", a term hitherto not even used in legal parlance. Domestic violence is defined in a comprehensive way in S.3 of the Act, comprising physical, mental, verbal, emotional psychological, sexual and economic abuse, harassment for dowry, acts of threatening to abuse the victim or any other person related to her.[19] Even a single act of commission or omission may constitute domestic violence. In other words, women do not have to suffer a prolonged period of abuse before taking recourse to the law.

Shared Household

As defined under Section 2(3) of the Act expression shared household means where the person aggrieved lives or at any stage has lived in a domestic relationship either singly or along with the respondent and includes a household whether owned or tenanted either jointly by the aggrieved and respondent or owned or tenanted by either of them in respect of which either of them or both have any right, title, equity or interest and includes such a household which may belong to the joint family of which the respondent is a member irrespective of whether the respondent or the aggrieved person has any title, right or interest in the shared household.[20]

Role of Indian Judiciary in the Protection of Women

It has been the prime objective of the judiciary to ensure that women are able to live securely in the society whether they are at home or at their working places. The meaning and content of the fundamental rights are of sufficient amplitude to encompass all the facets of gender equality. For instance in *Jaiveer v. Smt. Babita*[21] Allahabad high court held that deserted wife entititled to maintenance. Similarly, in *Kesuram v. Saraswati and others*[22] Supreme Court held that a wife who finds herself insecure in her husband's home and lives separately is entitled to maintenance. A very important case on the point is *Mohd. Ahmed Khan v.Shah Bano Begum*[23] in which Supreme Court held muslin women entitled to maintenance beyond the period of iddat if she is unable to maintain herself.

Moreover, in *Vishakha v, State of Rajasthan*[24] I was held by Supreme Court that protection of women from sexual harassment and right to work with dignity is a basic human right which is recognised universally. Domestic Violence Act 2005 is a step forward in protection of women, a significant attempt in India to recognise domestic abuse as a punishable offence and also to protect those women who are involved in live-in relationships. A huge number of cases have been decided under the Act. In *Anil Kumar v. Sindhu,*[25] Kerala High Court has held that Chapter XIII of Criminal Procedure Court 1973 is applicable to the proceedings under the Protection of Women from Domestic Violence Act, 2005. In *Nand Kishore v. State of Rajasthan,*[26] Jaipur bench of Rajasthan held that under proviso of Section 2(q) wife can file complaint against any male or female relative of the husband as the word used in the section is "relative" and this does not mean male relative only. In *S.Prabhakaran v.State of Kerala,*[27] Court held that wife has a right to live in the household whether it be the joint family house of the husband or the residential building of parents-in-law, if the wife lives or has at any stage lived in a domestic relationship either singly or along with the husband. In *Vishal Damodar Patil v.Vishakha Vishal Patil,*[28] Bombay High Court held that magistrate can order interim maintenance and no separate application is necessary for the same. However, opportunity of hearing has to be afforded to respondent before granting interim relief. In *S.R. Batra v. Smt. Taruna Batra,*[29] Supreme Court held that definition of 'shared household' used in Section 2(s) of the Act is not very happily worded and appears to be the result of clumsy drafting. In *Vandhana v. T. Srikanth*[30], it was held by Madras High Court that a wife during subsistence of marriage has a legal right to live in shared household even in the past she never resided in share household. In *Aruna Pramod Shah v. Union of India*[31] it is perfectly constitutional for Parliament to provide for protection to a woman in a relationship akin to marriage, along with and juxtaposed to the protection given to wives and legitimate children. Also, it was held that it is possibility of men becoming victims of domestic violence, but such cases would be few and far between and thus the Act cannot be challenged on the ground that it provides protection only to women and not men.

Fallacies in the Act

While the Domestic Violence Act has made improvements over existing laws but there are certain shortcomings in the Act. The law says -any definition of domestic violence must detail the fact that it is a human rights violation (may still be decided by Individual Judges).Law details the different forms of violence faced by women ......this may be theoretical exercise and may differ in practice. There is no mandatory sensitization of judges and law enforcement officials and still mental health component is not paid adequate dues.[32]

Misuse of the act, like all such acts in India, cannot be ruled out. In fact, with a system as corrupt as ours, money, clout and muscle power will always call the shots. And as long as the woman stays a puppet or pawn in the hands of her male relatives, she will always be manipulated and used.[33] The chances of the act being misused are enormous. We have seen in past how The Dowry Prohibition Act, 1961 has been misused from the side of the so-called aggrieved person.

Moreover, the definition of Domestic Violence is too wide. The Act says that "under the sole testimony of the aggrieved person, the court may conclude that an offence has been committed by the accused"[34] How can the court ensure that the complaints of the affected party is right or not. The presence of the malafide intentions on part of one party to harass the other cannot be ruled out.

In the definition of child it is not specified that whether the definition applies to male child or not as the very title of the Act indicates that it has been enacted to protect the rights of women. Yet, it must be kept in mind that domestic violence, though predominantly faced by women, be they wives, mothers, sisters or daughters, is also aimed against male children at times. It seems a poor excuse to say that male children should not be provided easily accessible relief from domestic violence simply because of their gender.

There is also a doubt as to whether this Act can be effectively implemented by the administrative bodies. Can the Police, Protection Officers and NGO's do there work efficiently.

Suggestions

There is no doubt that present enactment enjoys an important place in legal domain but certain improvements are, however, required. Some of the suggestions are as follows:

1. A balance should be maintained between other enactments and the Act as a women who is living in adultery is not entitled to maintenance and this is a valid ground of divorce but she is protected under this Act.
2. Under the Act, the sole testimony of the aggrieved person is sufficient and on that court may conclude that an offence has been committed by the accused but this should be proved as one may misuse this provision to embarrass and harass the respondent.
3. Male child should be included in the definition of aggrieved person as the child who is brought up in an environment of violence suffers a lot mentally.
4. Due concern should be given to mental health as this is something which is not visible to eyes but disturbs a lot.
5. Special judges should be appointed for speedy disposal of cases under the Act.
6. There should be an officer appointed to keep check on Police and Protection Officers to make sure they work efficiently.

Conclusion

Domestic violence can never be eliminated from society unless society refuses to tolerate it. This requires an internal change in the basic nature of Indian society, beginning with the recognition of the worth of every human being as an individual. If the law does not buck up in terms of implementing punishment on those who violate others within the sacred walls of the institution called family and home, the weaker will continue to be violated and abused by the stronger - physically, mentally, materially and spiritually.[35]

The Act, by and large, is a valuable piece of legislation. Its shortcomings do not, on final analysis; blot out the immense benefit the Act could be of to women. A good thing about the Act is the fact that it deals with domestic violence regardless of the religion of the parties.[36]

It is not that we do not have laws, we do have but we do not implement them properly and effectively to achieve desired results. Domestic violence is one of the grave and common crime against women so this is the time for women to stand and fight the battle for their dignity and individuality themselves else this important piece of legislation would go wasted.

Notes

1. Rai, Suman, Preface, *Law Relating to Protection of Women from Domestic Violence.* New Delhi, Orient, 2008, VII.
2. Fineman M.A and My. Kitiuk, eds., Preface, *The Public Nature of Private Violence: The Discovery of Domestic Abuse.* New York: Rutledge, 1994. XI-XVIII.
3. Rao, Mamta, *Law related to Women and Children,* Lucknow: Eastern, 2005. p. 152-153
4. Rai, Suman, *Law relating to Protection of Women from Domestic Violence,* New Delhi: Orient, 2008. p. 60.
5. *Ibid.* 61-67
6. 1981, 2(SCR) 516
7. 1997, 11(SCC) 123
8. 1996, 2(SCC) 549
9. Retrieved from *http://www.legalserviceindia.com/articles/dmt.htm.visited* on April 25, 2010.
10. Section 4 of the Protection of Women from Domestic Violence Act, 2005.
11. Section 8 of the Protection of Women from Domestic Violence Act, 2005.
12. Tripathi,S.C and Arora Vibha, *Law relating to Women and Children,* Allahabad:Central law Publications,2006.p45
13. Section 20 of the Protection of Women from Domestic Violence Act, 2005.
14. Section 20(2) of the Protection of Women from Domestic Violence Act, 2005.
15. Section 31 of the Protection of Women from Domestic Violence Act, 2005.
16. Rai, Suman, *Law relating to Protection of Women from Domestic Violence,* New Delhi, Orient, 2008. p. 22.

17. Tripathi,S.C and Arora Vibha, *Law relating to Women and Children*. Allahabad: Central Law Publications, 2006, p. 46.
18. *Ibid.*
19. Retrieved from *http://www.legalserviceindia.com/articles/dmt.htm.visited* on April 25, 2010.
20. Tripathi, S.C and Arora Vibha, *Law relating to Women and Children*. Allahabad, Central Law Publications, 2006, p. 46.
21. 1999 (2) JIC 117(All.)
22. 1997 Cr.L.J. 2525
23. 1985 (2) SCC 556
24. 1997 (6) SCC 247
25. 2009 (5) RCR (Criminal) 343 (Kerala)
26. 2009 (2) RCR (Criminal) 909 (Rajasthan)
27. 2009 (2) RCR (Civil) 883 (Kerala)
28. 2009 Cri LJ. 107 (Bombay)
29. AIR 2007 SC 1118
30. 2008(1) RCR (Civil) 366 (Madras)
31. 2008(3) RCR(Criminal) 192 (Delhi)
32. Parkar R. Shubhangi and Rupali Shivalkar , a brief on Psychiatry and the Law-Indian Scenario at Chennai presented at Midterm CME IPS on 16th-17th Aug. 2008.
33. Rattandeep kaur and Mona Goel," The Protection of Women from Domestic Violence Act, 2005: A Socio-Legal Study", *Law Journal of Guru Nanak Dev University*, Vol. XVII, 203-215.
34. Section 32(2) of the Protection of Women from Domestic Violence Act, 2005.
35. Retrieved from *http://www.domesticviolence.in.visited* on April 26,2010
36. Retrieved from *http://www.legalserviceindia.com/articles/dmt.htm.visited* on April 25, 2010.

CHALLENGES OF INDIAN WOMEN IN BPO INDUSTRY

P. Srinivas Subbarao[*] *& P. Suseela Rani*[**]

Today, India has more working women than any other country in the world. of the entire workforce of 400 million, 30-35 per cent is women, and of these, only 20 per cent work in urban India. This figure can largely be attributed to the growth of the BPO industry, which is one of the largest recruiters of a qualified workforce in recent times. In mid '80s, only 5-8 per cent of students in engineering colleges and approximately 5-30 per cent of the population entering the IT industry were women. By 2005, 40.4 per cent of the entrants into institutions of higher education were women. Women in IT workforce grew from 421,460 in 2006 to 670,984 in 2008, as per NASSCOM study. India has the largest number of women working in BPO's than any other single country in the world. This can be partly attributed to the growth of BPO's in India.

"The Indian IT-BPO industry has set high standard in gender inclusivity. Women are a key and vital part of our workforce, and their participation in the workforce is seen as a critical enabling factor for continued growth of the industry," said Sangeeta Gupta, VP, NASSCOM, who spoke on the occasion of the launch of the study report on Women in IT-BPO Industry.

BPO Industry in India

BPO entered the Indian Territory in the early 1990's. India is a unanimous choice across the globe due to the availability of a large amount of cheap but skilled manpower. The BPO industry

---

* *Head of the Department, Dept. of Management Studies, Commerce & HRM, M.R.P.G. College, Vizianagaram-535001, (E-mail: ss_pasumarti@yahoo.co.in)*

** *Associate Professor, Department of MBA, TRR College of Engineering & Technology, Hyderabad, AP*

stepped in to India with the entry of captive units of GE, HSBC, etc in 1992. India receives most of the outsourcing jobs from the USA. The US people have acknowledged that India is the best place for outsourcing. Indian employees have already proved their mettle by handling the jobs.

India is one of the prime beneficiaries of BPO. According to the Gartner Study; the Indian BPO segment is $2.4 bn against the world wide segment of $143 bn. Nasscom expects it to grow 15 fold in the next 6 years to an estimated size $21-24 bn. The advantage for India being the largest base for BPO is that they have a pool of highly competent and inexpensive English speaking graduates, high computer literacy rate and skilled quality conscious professionals.

Business process outsourcing (BPO) is a broad term referring to outsourcing in all fields. A BPO differentiates itself by either putting in new technology or applying existing technology in a new way to improve a process.

Business Process Outsourcing (BPO) is the delegation of one or more IT-intensive business processes to an external provider that in turn owns, administers and manages the selected process based on defined and measurable performance criteria. Business Process Outsourcing (BPO) is one of the fastest growing segments of the *Information Technology Enabled Services (ITES)* industry.

Women Force in Indian BPO Industry

Women are one of the driving forces behind the success of call center industry in India. The Indian BPO industry accounts for a revenue US$ 39.6 billion and has emerged as one of the largest private industry providing direct employment to 1.6 million professionals. The participation of women in BPO industry has been seen as a critical enabling factor for continued growth of the industry. Today BPO companies are recognizing women on board at all levels and this helps the organization to make good business sense. Therefore, BPO companies are trying to develop and involve women for higher roles and functions.

India has the largest number of women working in BPO' than any other single country in the world. This can be partly attributed to the growth of BPO's in India. It is a 28 billion dollar industry and with this beginning of the rural BPO units, it is thought to bring about a new wave of social revolution.

Women Employees in BPO in Some States

Name of the State	*Percentage of Women Employees*
Gujarat	60%
Andhra Pradesh	40%
Karnataka	40%
Rajasthan	31%
Maharastra	25.7%

Women in Indian Rural BPO Firms

The outlook for rural India is beginning to change. As the New York Times recently noted, a company called *Rural Shores* is taking outsourcing jobs to Indians living in rural India. Currently, Real Shores has three centers in operation but they aim to have 500 centers spread across India within the next five to seven years that will employ 100,000 rural Indian youth doing book keeping, bills processing, document scanning, data entry and other simple tasks that do not require English fluency as most rural Indians at best only speak basic English. It is a win-win scenario model.

Business Week, quoted *Wipro's Chairman* in 2007 saying that "it would be difficult to achieve international standards for service and to scale up village and rural based operations".

- Call center firms are found to include is their own location which is far from the other big cities in the rural communities and in the semi urban areas such as Munnar, Kerala, Ethakota in Andhra Pradesh and Shiggaon in Karnataka. Additionally, these are call center firms where more than half of the employees are found to be women and all of the employees are aged between 19 and 35.
- The country's biggest Software Services company Infosys, has joined hands with the rural development department in Andhra Pradesh to set up Rural BPOs in 22 districts that would create 1,000 fresh jobs, mainly for poor, educated, employable women.
- *AP is the First State* where such a project is being piloted in association with Desicrew Solutions Pvt. Ltd. and Ruralshores Business Services Pvt. Ltd.
- In the entire India, there are more than 100 call center units in operation in Rural areas.

Empowerment of Women Through BPO Industry

- Women especially in India have found out that, the wages that they earn through a BPO job help them to experience freedom and autonomy.
- Women are satisfied and enjoy their work at call centers.
- A call center job gives them more freedom and autonomy.
- Women are happy to learn new skills and have learnt to become more assertive.
- The acquired call center skills ranging from soft skills like communication, interpersonal and listening skills to product knowledge and technical knowledge have given a sense of confidence in women.
- This helps them to deal with customers as well as society at large.
- The interpersonal skills of women are now being recognized and valued in call centers.

- In most of the call centers, a premium is attached to women's voice and interpersonal skills.
- This is because the quality of customer care jobs ultimately helps a company to gain huge profits.
- The development of IT industry in India had a clear impact on emancipation of women.
- According to the studies of village pay phones in Bangladesh, advancement of computer aided technologies and networking in India show that the household income has increased and women have a say and mobility in household matters.
- Today women play a vital role as the part of the BPO workforce.

Challenges Faced by Women in BPO Industry

- In India the women mobility has always been controlled by men even in case of highly educated and independent women.
- With introduction of communication technologies and new information the workload of every woman has increased.
- They have to do the unpaid household chores in addition to the paid work in the BPO industry.
- There is no doubt that technology itself is gendered and is strongly shaped by the patriarchal yardstick of class and gender.
- The Indian BPO industry has set high standards in gender inclusivity.
- In many cases the women are forced to quit their jobs because of the disapproval of the husband and his family.
- There is a general lack of confidence among women at junior levels to speak up against issues such as "graveyard shifts" (night shifts).
- Lack of adequate safety and security measures.
- Exploitation of women is very much more in call centers.
- More physical stress is there.
- Mundane nature of the job and low status of call center work.
- The women are being subjected to sexual harassment verbally and physically by the bosses and colleagues in sophisticated hi-tech ways in BPO industry.
- The sexual harassment often follows with favours of increase in pay and by way of promotions by the bosses in B.P.O industry.
- Another survey on sexual harassment at the workplace by a NGO, centre for transforming India, in BPO sectors found that 88 per cent of 600 female employees questioned across the nations metros had suffered from of sexual

harassment, 47 per cent did not know how to report such incidents, and 50 per cent said that they faced abusive language and demands for sexual favours.

- A recent survey in the I.T & B.P.O. industry about sexual harassment in the metropolitan cites Bangalore, Pune, Mumbai, Delhi, Kolkata and Hyderabad revealed that women employees are often subjected to sexual harassment verbally and physically and that 40% of these harassments come from their bosses.
- Another recent survey conducted on sexual harassment of teenage girls in our non-metropolitan cities VIA online and I.T. instruments like cell-phones, it is revealed that this problem is widely spread across the states and actually is far higher in small cities and towns of this country.

Glass Ceiling

Glass ceiling is a word coined by Americans during early 1970's to describe the phenomena of societal and organizational prejudiced attitudes that create artificial barriers preventing women reaching senior executive positions.

The latest findings of a survey reveals that only a small number of women hold top positions in corporate houses worldwide, while in India only 14 per cent of women make it to the top management level. IT/ITES industry though employee women at a large percentage, but the percentage of women in top are quiets less. Women tend to be over representative in lower level job and under representative in the higher level of jobs in IT and ITES industry, The main reason why a men is preferred for top level post rather than a women- Many women are unable to put in as many hours as their male counterparts for many reasons, male employee complain that the deadline is not met by women employee, women also often find it difficulty to make up for the loss of experience and learning during maternity leave. Husband career affects women career. Networking is major issue among women as soon as they finish work they go home. Women marriage age is 25-30 after that they quit the job the age of 25-30 is too young to be given a top post. Male employees prefer to leave the job then to report to a women boss.

Women are becoming serious about assessing priority to their profession and they are able to break the glass ceiling in BPOs to some extent. Top women in IT/ITES industry:

Mrs. Padma Ravichandar - Perot Systems

Mrs. Neelam Dhawan - Microsoft

Mrs. Rekha Menon - Accenture

Mrs. Jessie Paul - Wipro

Mrs. Revathi Kasthuri - Novell India.

Work Life Balance

The term work life balance was coined in 1986, A good definition of Work-Life Balance is: Meaningful daily Achievement and Enjoyment in each of my four life quadrants: Work, Family, Friends and Self.

A research project, conducted in 9 cities, by avtar career creators, about the work life balance of Indian working women revealed the fact that more than 73% of the women interviewed felt that managing a home and a career was the primary reason for their stress and the resulting poor health. Inability to focus on one's own personal wellness, apportioning time for other activities such as gardening or other hobbies, becomes nearly impossible while juggling a demanding career and a home.

The strategy of employing part-time or flexi-time workers is one, which Corporate India is slowly but surely testing out. Companies such as the Pantaloon Group, Unilever India Shares Services, Scope International, Barclays Bank, Cap Gemini, the Murugappa Group, Tata VSNL and several other FMCG, Telecom and IT companies have successfully implemented the Flexi-Career concept in their organizations.

Some Nasty Incidents on Women Working in BPO Industry

1. Shivakumar, then 22, had raped and murdered Pratibha, 28, in Anjanapura Layout on the night of December 13, 2005, after picking her up from home to ferry her to HP Global Soft, a BPO where she was doing night shifts. Although it took four years and 10 months for the judgment in the Pratibha murder case to be delivered, investigating officers had nailed the accused within a week of the incident. At last, The judgment, which was pronounced recently, sentenced the killer Shivakumar to life imprisonment till death.
2. On the night of Nov 23, 2010, a 30-year-old BPO staffer - a native of Mizoram-was abducted by five men and gang raped in a moving goods carrier in the capital.

   She was abducted soon after she and another woman were dropped 100 metres from her home by her office vehicle in Dhaula Kuan area of south Delhi late at night. The men then drove all the way to Mongolpuri in north Delhi and dumped her there after raping her.
3. New Delhi: A 30-year-old woman, working with a BPO in Gurgaon, was allegedly gang raped by five men after being abducted from outside her house in Dhaula Kuan, the Delhi Police made sketches of the suspects on the basis of descriptions provided by the victim and her friend. The victim, who hails from the Northeast, told the police that she was assaulted by five men who appeared to be aged between 20 and 25. Though they didn't sound educated, some of them used English words to abuse and intimidate her, the woman told the police.

4. *Chennai BPO date rape case-Thu., Aug. 07, 2008 10:45:41 IST:*A call centre employee with a prominent BPO in Chennai was arrested few days back on charges of drugging and then raping his female colleague. This, however, seems to be a case of loose lifestyle practices and its eerie aftermath.

   A CALL centre based crime that came to light a few days ago from Chennai, exposing an alleged rape attempt by a call centre trainer, has once again brought to the fore the fact that all is not well with this 24x7 employment environment. Considering the number of educated girls finding employment in Business Process Outsourcings (BPOs), incidents like these may not raise many eyebrows. Still, it is worth noting here that something is fishy in this professional sphere

5. *Manipuri girl, a BPO employee gang raped in capital:* New Delhi, Nov 25: Once again BPO employee became the victim of gangrape in New Delhi at midnight on Nov 24. A 30-year-old Manipuri girl was abducted and raped while returning from job. The victim was dropped by her office cab near her house at 1AM. She was allegedly abducted by a group of people and was raped in a moving car.

The accused, who are still absconding, later left the girl in a secluded place in semi-conscious state. However, police claimed, "The victim's abduction does not seem planned. Since the cab dropped her at a secluded spot the criminals seem to have struck sensing her helplessness."

Necessary Methods to Overcome Above Challenges/problems

- BPO companies have tightened their safety policies.
- Company-sponsored pick-up and drop vehicles have been provided for women employees.
- Company rules must stipulate that women must travel only in the presence of another male employee.
- Internal hotlines and SMS services have been introduced to monitor the well-being of commuting employees.
- Adequate background checks on the designated cab drivers are also made by the employers.
- These measures have improved the situation considerably, though it still does not make the women employees feel 100% safe, especially when they work in night shifts.
- The government, on its part, can make it mandatory for companies to install GPS in cabs to have a stronger monitoring.
- Self-defense training to women.
- Installing CCTVs at the workplace to prevent sexual harassment.
- Police verification of cab drivers, security guards and peons working in BPOs.

- Efficient complaint redressal systems should be made compulsory for all employers.
- Implement Anti-harassment policy in all BPOs.
- Arrange Healthcare and awareness programs.
- Arrange Women's lounge and recreational activities.

Conclusion

Globally, 60% of those employed in this sector are women. In India, however, the percentage is 35. But the industry believes this can go up to 50 per cent if labour laws are modified. The social evil of sexual harassment is spreading due to the lack of any legislation of structural safe-guards in our country. So, *'Protection of Women Against Sexual Harassment at the Work Place Bill -2010'* was passed by The UPA Government. This bill will help in achieving empowerment of women and women's rights of gender equality to life, liberty and equality of women in working conditions everywhere.

The BPO companies needed to have an internal code to ensure security of women employees and take measures to ensure they discharge their job in a secure atmosphere. It also recommended that the government needed to make it mandatory for companies to install Global Positioning System (GPS) in cabs, not only in call centers and BPO's but all industries which engage women in night shifts. Other measures that can be taken include providing self defense training to women; installing safety devices at the work place; undertaking police verification of cab drivers, security guards and peons who are deputed on night shifts and setting up efficient complaint redressal systems.

References

http://www.bpoindia.org/research/bpo-in-india.shtml

http://www.articlesbundle.com/Art/76045/559/Women-Employees-In-BPO.html

http://www.paycheck.in/main/work-and-pay/women-paycheck/articles/challenges-facing-women-working-in-call-centres-and-bpos.

http://www.iloveindia.com/economy-of-india/bpo-industry.html

http://outsourceportfolio.com/growing-women-employees-indian-bpo/ (growing Women employee in Indian BPO)

http://hubpages.com/hub/Women-employees-in-Indian-Rural-BPO-firms (rural employment)

http://www.nasscom.in/upload/68117/NASSCOM-Mercer-Gender-Inclusivity-Report.pdf (Nasscom)

http://www.educationtimes.com/educationTimes/CMSD/Walk-A-Job/27/20110301201103011723282648a23b17a/Caution-Women-at-work.html

http://outsourceportfolio.com/bpo-providing-indias-rural-poor-opportunity

http://www.classstruggle.in/dec/sexual.html

http://www.rediff.com/money/2005/jun/15bpo.htm (Gujarat)

http://www.hindu.com/2010/11/30/stories/2010113063501300.htm(Karnataka).

INTIMATE PARTNER VIOLENCE: THE GLARING REALITY

Fatima Quraishi[*] *& Isha Khurana*[*]

Domestic violence against women and girls is an undisputed fact and it is widely accepted phenomenon. The violence perpetrated against females is due to the male dominant society but, what is less widely recognized is violence against men and boys which is on a rise. With the growth in the economy, better standards of living and change in societal attitude, the aggression against males is gradually on the rise.

The U. S. Office on Violence against Women (OVW) defines domestic violence as a "pattern of abusive behavior in any relationship that is used by one partner to gain or maintain power and control over another intimate partner". The definition adds that domestic violence "can happen to anyone regardless of race, age, sexual orientation, religion, or gender", and that it can take many forms, including physical abuse, sexual abuse, emotional, economic, and psychological abuse.[1]

Intimate partner violence leads to violations of basic human rights. The concept of human rights evolved largely from ideas of western political theory about rights of individuals to autonomy and freedom. Thus the law evolved to protect individuals' autonomy vis-a-vis the state and it held States responsible for individual rights and accountable for abuse of the same. In due course of time the scope of State's responsibility has expanded to include not only the abuse directly committed by itself or by its agents, but also state's systematic failure to prosecute the actions committed by its agents or private individuals. This implies that though the State or its agents may not be responsible for the acts of violence, its failure to prosecute the abuse was held as amounting to complicity in it.

---

* *3rd year students of Dr. Ram Manohar Lohia National Law University, Lucknow.*

The definition of domestic violence so given by the U.S. Office on Violence against Women is also gender neutral in nature. The principle of non-discrimination has been correctly described as fundamental to the concept of human rights. It is specifically affirmed, for example, in the Preamble to the United Nations Charter, the Universal Declaration of Human Rights, 1948 (UDHR)[2]and the InternationalCovenant on Civil and Political Rights, 1966 (ICCPR)[3]. The male victims are being discriminated against their female counterparts just because of our patriarchal mind set. It is an undisputed fact that violence on females is more in comparison to males but the possibility of males being aggrieved cannot be ruled out and hence, they should be provided with adequate safeguards.

International Perspective

Many international organizations - UN agencies, governmental and intergovernmental organizations, NGOs, international criminal courts - have acknowledged the issue in their publications and their members have shown a high degree of individual sensitization and concern. Nevertheless, it has not been embedded in any legal code. Media and the politics have continuously and purposely marginalize the male victims. This is a form of discrimination by omission which further leads to human rights violation of male victims.

Researches in various countries indicate that a cohort of men suffer from similar kind of violence inflicted on them by their partners. Despite an increasing awareness that domestic violence is a significant public health issue, little is known about domestic violence committed by women against men internationally.

There are a few reasons, .i.e., firstly, there is no universally accepted definition of what constitutes domestic violence against men (even against women[4]). Secondly, it is not always possible to identify whether male victims of domestic violence are purely victims, or abusers who have been assaulted back by their victims.

Types of Intimate Relationship Violence

Females are provided with protection by various municipal and international legislations such as Convention on the Elimination of Discrimination Against Women (CEDAW) but there are no such legislations for males. The quandary of male-directed violence is not unknown to the humanitarian community but bringing it to light is a major issue which needs to be addressed.

Partner violence cannot be understood without acknowledging important distinctions among types of violence, motives of perpetrators, the social location of both the partners, and the cultural contexts in which violence occurs. Battering, a word commonly used for such kind of violence occurs in gay male couples, lesbian couples and heterosexual women who physically assault the males.

The four major patterns of violence[5] are:

Common Couple Violence (CCV)

This is identified as a general pattern of control. It arises in specific argument where both partners lash out on each other physically. It has lower per-couple frequency as compared to IT, not likely to escalate over time, is not likely to involve severe violence and is more likely to be mutual.

Intimate Terrorism (IT)

The violence in such cases is motivated by a wish to exert general control over one's partner. It involves more per couple incidents of violence than CCV, is more likely to escalate over time and is less likely to be mutual and is more likely to involve serious injury.

Violent Resistance (VR)

This terminology is preferred over 'self defence' because the latter term is defined under law. According to research VR is perpetrated almost always by women.

Mutual Violent Control (MVR)

This is a couple pattern where both husband and wife are controlling and violent, in a situation that can be viewed as two intimate terrorists battling for control.

International Dossier

A recent 32-nation study revealed that more than 51% of men and 52% of women felt that there were times when it was appropriate for a wife to slap her husband.[6]An Australian study indicated that 15.5% of men attending an emergency department had experienced domestic violence at some point in their life, about half that of women in the same study.[7] Male victims account for 48.6% of the total victims of force in England and Wales.[8] As per a survey done in Canada, 44% of Domestic Violence victims are men.[9] It was further opined that in present scenario Canadian men were more likely to be victims of domestic violence.

UK Home Office Research Centre revealed that each year, 834,000 men are raped or physically assaulted by intimate partners an average of 3.5 times a year, for a total of 2.9 million assaults around the world per year.[10]

Further, in a study undertaken by the Home office of UK it was concludedthat 63% of male chronic and 80% of male intermittent victims stated that assaults experienced were 'just something that happens'. Only 6% and 1% respectively saw it as a crime against them.[11] Supplementing, it was instituted that 49% of the men never sought help from the police, since they felt that the police would be unsympathetic or indeed disbelieve them.[12]

Legal protections given to women have been designed to serve as weapons for legal harassment of men. There have been numerous incidents where the women have tried to exploit their spouses behind the veil of Domestic Violence legislations.

The Native Story

Due to the presence of a patriarchal society in India, all men are branded as *"batterers"* and all women as *"victims"*. It is because of this male dominated society that it is considered that only females can be the victims of the domestic violence. The idea of female being the perpetrators of the offence of intimate partner violence is just alien to the Indian society. Protection of Women against Domestic Violence Act, 2005 (PWDVA) was enacted to protect females.

The legislation so enacted in India against the offence of domestic violence is based on feminist approach. It provides protection only to the fairer sex. There are no such legislations to shield males from similar kind of violence.

Legal Potency of PWDVA, 2005

This biasness of the legislature in framing Protection of Women against Domestic Violence Act, 2005 was challenged many a times for being violative of Article 14 of the Constitution of India. The Delhi High Court in a recent decision[13] dismissed the petition saying that the argument held no merit as the court was of the view that, *"Though men are victims of violence, such incidences are few and far between, thus ruling out the possibility of protection for men from the parliament."* The above statement, reflects a very sad story, which though acknowledges the existence of domestic violence against men, but refuses to accept it due to lack of data to substantiate the claim.

Another remarkable case is of *Dennison Paulraj and Ors. v. Union of India and Ors.*[14] decided in the year 2009 where it was contended that under the said Act, the husband cannot file any application against violence and it is the statutory right of only the wife. This was challenged on the basis of being violative of Article 14 and Article 21 of the Constitution of India. It was held that such discrimination acceptably falls under Article 15(3)[15] and cannot be said to be infringing Article 14 or Article 16 of the Constitution.

This case is important in the sense that today when women have come up in a big way and made a mark for themselves globally then why they need biased law for their upliftment. It is high time to voice forgender neutral laws. Females take advantage of the special privilege accorded to them by law on one hand and on the other hand ask for equal treatment in all walks of life. These are double standards which have to be taken care of immediately.

Misuse of Welfare Legislation

The legal code so designed for protection women has been highly misused. There have been a number of cases where females have attempted to jeopardize the social standing of their husbands. In this respect the court rightly held in the case of *Gaurav Gupta v. Nidhi Bansal & Ors*[16] that wife hadno legal right to tarnish the image of her husbandor affect his social standing by making false accusation against him, particularly when those accusations have the potential of jeopardizing the employment of the plaintiff.

Women are also capable of causing economic damage to men under the garb of claiming maintenance and compensation for the so called mental agony. In *Amit Khanna v. Priyanka Khanna*[17] it was held that the mere allegations made by the wife that husband was owner of vast movable and immovable properties does not give court the jurisdiction to the Court to pass an order of maintenance beyond the means of the husband and such claims need to be proved by clear and substantial evidence.

The claim for additional maintenance by amalgamating Section 125 of Criminal Procedure Code (Cr.P.C) and PWDVA were out rightly rejected by the court in the case of *Rachna Kathuria v. Ramesh Kathuria*[18]. It was held that PWDVA does not create any additional right to claim maintenance on the part of the aggrieved person.

In a Rajasthan High Court case[19] it was held that filing of frivolous complaints against the spouse amounts to cruelty which gives him or her right to seek divorce. Another interesting case where the cause of man was recognized was the case of *Sanjay Bhardwaj & Ors. v. The State & Anr*[20] where it was said that an unemployed husband cannot be held liable to pay maintenance.

'We are living in an era of equality of sexes. The Constitution provides equal treatment to be given irrespective of sex, caste and creed. An unemployed husband, who is holding an MBA degree, cannot be treated differently to an unemployed wife, who is also holding an MBA degree. Since both are on equal footing one cannot be asked to maintain other unless one is employed and other is not employed. As far as dependency on parents is concerned, I consider that once a person is grown up, educated he cannot be asked to beg and borrow from the parents and maintain wife. The parents had done their duty of educating them and now they cannot be burdened to maintain husband and wife as both are grown up and must take care of themselves.'

J. Dalveer Bhandari in the case of *Preeti Gupta & Another v. State of Jharkhand & Another*[21] said that frivolous complaints have caused social unrest. Quoting as follows:

'The criminal trials lead to immense sufferings for all concerned. Even ultimate acquittal in the trial may also not be able to wipe out the deep scars of suffering of ignominy. Unfortunately a large number of these complaints have not only flooded the courts but also have led to enormous social unrest affecting peace, harmony and happiness of the society. It is high time that the legislature must take into consideration the pragmatic realities and make suitable changes in the existing law. It is imperative for the legislature to take into consideration the informed public opinion and the pragmatic realities in consideration and make necessary changes in the relevant provisions of law. We direct the Registry to send a copy of this judgment to the Law Commission and to the Union Law Secretary, Government of India who may place it before the Hon'ble Minister for Law & Justice to take appropriate steps in the larger interest of the society.'

The discussion of the above few cases clearly show the apathy of males in the present times. They are put behind bars and tortured unnecessary on the basis of inane complaints. The conviction rate of domestic violence cases is also very low. The females who subject their husbands to frivolous torture are set free without being prosecuted. This is also one form of abuse of man and his family where they are treated disrespectfully and forced into court for no rhyme or reason. Women have misused this protection time and again and a so called right of the man in domestic relation is deeply affected.

Male Bashing Statistics

The National Crime Records Bureau does not even maintain a separate heading for Domestic Violence against men[22]. In the current age where heinous crimes are being committed in huge numbers, violence against men is seen as a softer issue which does not require much mention. We can postpone its importance for sometime but neglect would not solve the issue by itself. It has to be deliberated upon and statutory provisions have to be enacted for its protection. The problem is in its nascent stage and can be effectively curtailed. The laid back attitude for protection of men against Domestic Violence has to be amended. All issues, big or small have to be given their required importance. It is of paramount significance that in a developing economy like India where males are usually the bread earners of the family, decent protection be given to them. Lack of statistical data does not mar the importance of the glaring reality that men are also subject to Domestic Violence. Indian laws have been notoriously used by females for economic advantage. 99 per cent of the cases of Domestic Violence and dowry harassment filed against men and their families are false and filed with a motive to extort money and unfortunately, the horse-trading goes on in the Court and is passed off as women liberation and empowerment of the weaker sex.

NGO's like Save Family Foundation and My Nation Foundation[23] conducted an online survey between April 2005 and March 2006 and found that out of 100,000 men surveyed during that one year, 98% of men faced severe Domestic Violence at the hands of their wives and in-laws in the form verbal, physical, emotional, mental and financial abuse.

1. Economic violence was the commonest, faced by 32.8% of participants.
2. Physical Violence was the closest second at 25.2%.
3. Emotional Violence followed suit at 22.2%.
4. While sexual violence contended fourth with 17.7%.
5. Verbal abuse was a problem faced by all men in the above categories.

Further investigation into the problem revealed that many such men who are unable to withstand domestic abuse, withdraw from the society, fell prey to addictions or in extreme cases end their own lives.

Conclusion

What we fail to understand here is that there has been a serious role reversal of the perpetrator of violence and the victim of violence, wherein the victim, being hailed as the criminal, is forced to compensate the tormentor, being hailed as the victim. But sadly enough, this trend is catching on slowly.

It looks highly delirious for a man to exist in a society suffering from double standards where one judgment speaks of the inability of the ambit of the Domestic Violence Act 2005 to cover men as victims and other one says that incidences of Domestic Violence being far and few between, men should not expect protection from the parliament. The raison d'être for the growing apathy and hatred against men in the society is the spread of radical feminist thinking in every sphere of public life, including the drafting of policies and laws.

It is not hard to see the repercussions of such differentiated similarities amongst men, who are now not even refraining from taking the law into their hands by either committing suicide or murder, what with having exasperated with the apathy meted out by the administrators of their own brethren.

There is a need of advocacy and support to encourage men to report Domestic Violence. There should be investment in resources to address the issues of domestic abuse and violence against men. Comprehensive data is required to help the victims of male bashing which should be prepared by the Governmental Authorities.

It is important that gender neutral laws are encouraged. A holistic approach should be adopted to maintain and nurture relationships especially marriage. Abuse of men though in small numbers does happen and should not be ignored. Proper protection should be accorded and general public should be sensitized to the need of the man today.

Legal protections given to women have been designed to serve as weapons for legal harassment of men. Once again this question is put forward to the civil society and the government that is radical feminism harming the society as a whole and affecting the institution of marriage negatively?

Notes

1. *'About Domestic Violence'*, United States Department of Justice [online] retrieved from <*http://www.ovw.usdoj.gov/domviolence.htm*> accessed on 10/02/2011.
2. Articles 2 and Article 7 of Universal Declaration of Human Rights 1948.
3. Articles 2(1), Article 3 & Article 26 of International Covenant on Civil and Political Rights, 1966.
4. Boyle A, Robinson S, Atkinson P, *'Domestic Violence in Emergency Medicine Patients'* Emerg Med J 2004; 21(1) 9-13.

5. Johnson Micheal P., Ferraro Kathleen J., '*Research on Domestic Violence in the 1990s: Making Distinctions*', *Journal of Marriage and Family*, Vol. 62, No. 4 (Nov., 2000), page 948-963 retrieved from *http://www.jstor.org/stable/1566718* accessed on 12/02/2011.

6. Watson Bruce, '*A Hidden Crime: Domestic Violence Against Men Is a Growing Problem*' retrieved from *http://www.dailyfinance.com/story/a-hidden-crime-domestic-violence-against-men-is-a-growing-probl/19297449/?icid=sphere_copyright*> accessed on 13/02/2011.

7. Roberts GL, O'Toole BI, Raphael B, Lawrence JM, Ashby R., '*Prevalence study of domestic violence victims in an emergency department*'. Ann Emerg Med 1996; 27(6):741-53 retrieved from <*http://www.hkcem.com/html/publications/Journal/2006-4/p212-216.pdf*> accessed on 20/02/2011.

8. Homicides, Firearm Offences and Intimate Violence (2005/2006) retrieved from <*http://rds.homeoffice.gov.uk/rds/pdfs07/hosb0207.pdf*> accessed on 18/02/2011.

9. Hoff Bert H.,' *Family Violence n Canada*' (2001) retrieved from <*http://www.batteredmen.com/batrcan.htm*> *and* <*http://www.statcan.gc.ca/pub/85-224-x/85-224-x2000000-eng.pdf*> accessed on 18/02/2011.

10. Ubudy Widyan Al, '*Battle of the Sexes: Violence Against Men*' retrieved from <*http://www.suite101.com/content/battle-of-the-sexes-violence-against-men-a332796#ixzz1EEwSbTpx* > accessed on 16/02/2011.

11. Mirrlees-Black Catriona, 'Domestic Violence: Findings from a new British Crime Survey self-completion questionnaire.' retrieved from <*http://rds.homeoffice.gov.uk/rds/pdfs/hors191.pdf*> accessed on 15/02/2011.

12. Browne Dr. Kevin, '*Dispatches:* 'Battered Men' Survey (1998)', retrieved from <*http://www.dewar4research.org/docs/bms2.pdf*> accessed on 22/02/2011.

13. *Aruna Parmod Shah* Vs. *Union of Indian* (Writ Petition (Crl.) No. 425 of 2008).

14. (Writ Petition No. 28521 of 2008 and M.P. No. 1 of 2008).

15. See Article 15 (3) of the Constitution of India states: "nothing in this Article shall prevent the State from making any special provision for women and children".

16. *Gaurav Gupta v. Nidhi Bansal & ors.* CS(OS) No.1772/2010.

17. (Crl. M.C. No. 4066 of 2009 & Crl. M.A. No. 13807/2009) decided on 01.09.2010.

18. (Crl.M.C.No. 130/2010).

19. *Smt.Anita Jain v. Rajendra Kumar Jain* D.B.CIVIL MISC. APPEAL No.45/2000.

20. (Crl.M.C.No. 491/2009)

21. Para 35 of Crl.M.C.No.1512 OF 2010.

22. 'Figures at a Glance: 2009', National Criminal Record Bureau retrieved from *http://ncrb.nic.in/CII-2009-NEW/cii-2009/figure%20at%20a%20glance.pdf* accessed on 22/02/2011.

23. Dhulia Viraj, '*Fact sheet on domestic violence against men in India*' retrieved from *http://aimwa.in/fact-sheet-on-domestic-violence-against-men-in-india* accessed on 20/02/2011.

HONOUR CRIMES-ATROCIOUS WOMEN VICTIMIZATION BY THE SHIELDERS OF THE SOCIAL AND CULTURAL REPUTES: AN INTERNATIONAL PERSPECTIVE

Jyothi Vishwanath & Srinivas C. Palakonda***

Introduction

The tendency of inflicting terrible violence upon the female population and massacring them physically and mentally for protecting the culture and social honour cuts across the racial, religious, cultural and regional divides of globe. Guardians of the social assumptions, culture, traditions and family reputation unhesitatingly and unreasonably regulate and control their conduct, behaviour and life. Whenever found at the cross roads with the accepted social and cultural ethical norms of a given social set-up, they are targeted. Ignoring and overlooking the value of a human life, overriding the sacred international human rights instruments settled after great discussions and deliberations for protecting the weaker sex from torture and violence, the perpetrators of culture crimes have perpetuated their horrendous acts of victimizing women with much greater force and confidence. Honour crimes are rapidly engulfing the entire ocean of mankind. Amidst this scenario, this paper undertakes to decipher the notion of honour as conceptualized in the modern societies; seeks to assess the magnitude of honour crimes, their nature and impact in the Asian and the western world; briefly reviews the prevalent legal and social approach towards these crimes and suggests the efforts mandatory from all the concerned quarters.

---

* *Assistant Professor, Post Graduate Department of Studies in Law & University Law College, Bangalore University, Bangalore.*

** *Assistant Professor, K.L.E.Society's Law College, Bangalore.*

Perceiving Honour in Relation to Woman

Honour is the most cherished value in the Indian sub-continental patriarchal families irrespective of the caste, regional and religious identities. Families gain and lose honour through money, power and the proper and improper behavior of their women. Actions appropriate according to *dharma* maintain the purity and honour of the family, lineage and caste while inappropriate actions defile it (Chakravarti, 2003:148-149). The ideology of honour, *i.e., izzat* is a gendered notion in India. Being the repository of such honour in the capacity of a daughter, wife and mother, greatest threat to it vests in her personality, body and conduct. Being the passive recipient of the male seed, she risks it by her shameful physical conduct. Whole notion of honour revolves around this social perception of the man's creative ability (Chowdhary, 2007:16-17). Since she represents fertility and growth, separate from the male and not under his control, her power is seen as dangerous, malevolent and potentially a destructive force (Dewan, 2000:35). The essential and innate nature of women, identified with her sexuality and represented as sinful, necessitates male control for preserving patrilineal property and caste hierarchy.

Much similar to the notions prevailing in the Indian sub-continent, honour shares close nexus with woman in other parts of the world. Table 1 analyses the concept of honour as perceived in the different multi-cultural societies like Jordan, Pakistan, Lebanon, Egypt, Palestine, Israel, Iraq, Italy and other countries.

Table 1
Perception of Honour

Honour and Woman	• Family, tribe, clan, community & conjugal honour vests in woman, her body, conduct & behaviour as prescribed by the patriarchal norms of ownership. • Woman's honour is property of her male relatives & she is merely its custodian & is bound to safeguard it for the sake of her family. • Families & communities in all civilizations & cultures have tried to regulate sexual behaviour of females (Welchman & Hossain, 2005:xi, 6). • Neo-Nazi group in UK holds that *'to live by honour means that one is prepared to die rather than be dishonoured'* (Welchman & Hossain, 2005:43-44).
Actions of woman bringing dishonour	• Associating with male friends, attending college or working without permission of family male elders, violating dress codes, choosing one's own life partner, losing virginity, adultery, refusing an arranged marriage or adjustment in an arranged marriage, falling in love with inappropriate person, dating with males, being caught in sexual activity, decision to seek divorce, engaging in extra-marital & pre-marital relationships, pregnancy from illegitimate sexual relations, marriage without family's knowledge/approval, expressing desire to marry against family wishes, prostitution, refusing sexual relations in a forced

	marriage, inter-religious marriage, complaining to police about violence, rumors of relations with men, living behaviour, leaving home frequently. • In Egypt, laughing loudly in public street, enjoying talking to a male stranger, talking to a male colleague in street, coming home late, leaving house without husband's consent, dressing inappropriately according to the male standards, being a victim of rape are deemed to bring dishonour.
Women's behaviour upholding honour	• Modest sexual behaviour • Avoiding contacts with men outside family in situations having any sexual potential • Preserving virginity for the husband • Fidelity in marriage • No pre-marital or extra-marital relationships with men • No unwarranted links with men outside the family • Meeting all familial obligations in the capacity of wife, mother, daughter & daughter-in-law towards husband, children, parents & parents-in-law respectively.

Thus it can be categorically said that though both women and men embody notions of family honour, the former is its repository while the latter is its regulator.

Nature and Impact of Honour Crimes in the Asian and the Western Societies

Honour crime is the killing of a woman by a male family member for engaging in or being suspected of engaging in sexual practices before or outside marriage (Welchman & Hossain, 2005:5). It includes any act of violence and abuse, actual or threatened, perpetrated against individuals, mainly women, by male members of the family and community in defence of their honour. Honour killings refer to the murder of a woman by her male relatives for a perceived violation of the social norms of sexuality, even if this is only a matter of rumor, gossip or being seen with a particular man (Zuhur, p. 22). It indicates the regulatory mechanisms comprising different types of manifest violent behaviour against women deemed to have defiled family's honour.

Being repository of family and caste honour, woman is simultaneously rendered an object of protection and violence. Fear of losing it makes men rationalize and justify masculine aggression and violence against her, thereby leading to wide acceptance and legitimization of violence against her in the family atmosphere. Such violence, not being purely private in nature, has a public face since it occurs in response to the cultural expectations of the larger community (Chowdhary, 2007: 17-18).

Providing exact statistics of honour killings is impossible in the absence of reliable methods of verifying and measuring its incidence. According to the United Nations High Commissioner for Human Rights, annually there are around 5000 instances of women and girls being shot, stoned, burned, buried alive, strangulated, smothered, knifed to death by fathers, brothers, sons, uncles, mothers for preserving family honour [Chaudhry, D.R (2010, August 1)].

The joint study conducted by London based CIMEL (Centre for Islamic and Middle Eastern Law) School of Oriental and African Studies and INTERIGHTS (The International Centre for the Legal Protection of Human Rights) in many Asian countries like India, Pakistan, Bangladesh, Nepal, Sri Lanka; Arab countries like Egypt, Iraq, Jordan, Kuwait, Lebanon, Libya, Syria and Tunisia; China, Japan, Brazil, Australia, UK, USA and others highlights that nexus between honour and violence on women permeates the eastern and western societies equally (Chowdhary, 2007:21-22).

India

Violation of the marriage codes is regarded as an attack upon *izzat* (Welchman & Hossain, 2005:8). Contentious marriages violating the norms of caste endogamy, territorial exogamy, religious endogamy, widow remarriage and gotra exogamy have mainly led to honour crimes in India, more particularly in Northern Indian belt including Haryana, Uttar Pradesh and other areas dominated by the Khap Panchayats. *Anuloma* and *pratiloma* marriages are always contested and criminalized.

Punishment for violations of endogamous and exogamous rules is excommunication from caste, killing of the mother and child or the married couple and even sometimes ritual death (Chakravarti, 2003:68; Banerjee-Dube, 2008:71). The rules of excommunication are very horrifying since no one dares to dine, drink, transact economically with the outcaste; the barber refuses to shave him; the *Brahman* refuses to officiate religious functions for him; no man would marry his children and the attendants of the dead would refuse to perform the funeral rites for him and his family members (Banerjee-Dube, 2008:71).

Whenever a young couple elopes after marriage or for marrying, the girl's family tries to criminalize their action and contest the validity of their marriage. It is alleged that the girl is a minor or insane and charges of kidnapping or abduction, wrongful confinement or rape are filed against her husband or lover and many times his family members are also implicated for harassing them. The woman is also pressurized to support the case of kidnapping. For loss of their family's honour, honour of the offending family is attacked. These measures are usually resorted to force the married couple to surface or to withdraw from such marriage. After they surface, in majority of the cases, they run the risk of humiliation, physical injury, assault, death, mental torture, interference with their choice in marriage (Welchman & Hossain, 2005:4), cruel decisions of caste panchayats. Death penalty is regarded a valid method of retrieving their lost honour. Sometimes the woman is solitarily confined or is sent to the state run protective homes raising legal issues of her custody (Welchman & Hossain, 2005:308-330).

In many cases she is forced into a greatly compromised marriage with a person who is either a widower, old man, a man with children or a handicapped man, a drunkard, not matching her educational qualifications or a fit for nothing person, after which the family cuts off all connections with her (Chowdhary, 2007: 10-11).

It is considered extremely necessary to bring back and punish her for re-establishing the family honour. She cannot be disowned. Her absorption into the traditional biradari network is difficult. Her physical elimination is an easier and honourable option open to the family than her forced or severely compromised marriage or remarriage in an inferior household. The blemish can be removed only by extinguishing the object of dishonour.

Other Asian and Western Societies

Table 2 displays the nature and impact of honour crimes in the Asian and western countries like Pakistan, Bangladesh, Nepal, Sri Lanka, Egypt, Iraq, Jordan, Kuwait, Lebanon, Libya, Syria, Tunisia, China, Japan, Brazil, Australia, UK, USA etc.

Table 2

Nature and Impact of Honour Crimes in the Asian and Western Societies

<table>
<tr><td>Purpose of honour crimes</td><td colspan="2">• Restoring & preserving lost honour of the family, clan, tribe & community
• For deterring, apprehending & intimidating the woman
• For intimidating other female members of the concerned society</td></tr>
<tr><td>Victims of honour crimes</td><td colspan="2">• Being dependent on men, whether fathers, husbands or sons, for the most basic requirements of life, women is the primary victim (Edwards, 1985:183).
• Even men are targets. In the Karo-kari honour killings in the province of Sindh in Pakistan, around 97 men were killed along with 158 women. In matters of forced marriages & interference with the right of choosing the time of marriage & marital partner, men are equally pressurized (Welchman & Hossain, 2005:6).</td></tr>
<tr><td>Perpetrators</td><td colspan="2">• Brothers, fathers, husband, son, nephew, paternal or maternal uncles, grandfathers, kinsmen & maternal female relatives.</td></tr>
<tr><td colspan="3">Two ways of restoring lost honour of the family</td></tr>
<tr><td rowspan="2">Actions which allegedly restore the lost honour i.e., honour crimes</td><td>Modification of transgressor's (woman) behaviour</td><td>Erasure of the carrier (woman) of honour</td></tr>
<tr><td>• Forced marriage
• Coerced marriage to an alleged rapist
• Mental or sexual harm (Welchman & Hossain, 2005:24).
• Intimidation, coercion, threats of force, withdrawal of family benefits & security
• Tightly controlling movements & conduct like time of coming home, smoking, drinking, kinds of dresses to be worn
• Monitoring, restricting & controlling friendships, conversations, choice of</td><td>• Killing.
• Forcing her to commit suicide.
• Public killing
Method of Elimination
• Burning to death [Pandey, Sanjay (2010, July 20)].
• Burying alive, stoning, pushing in the well,</td></tr>
</table>

	marriage partners, time of marriage • Unlawful confinement • Mutilation & disfigurement • Chopping of body parts like nose, hair [Brutal Justice: Pak Woman loses nose, hair to extramarital affair. (2010, November 30)] & other organs.	poisoning, shooting, stabbing, strangulation, drowning, beheading & hanging
Reflecting patriarchal attitude	• Legal codes & judicial decisions of different countries exempt and excuse the criminal & offer scope for mitigating the sentence.	

Apart from sharing similar notions of honour and dishonour, aforementioned countries resort to similar resultant actions against the violating woman irrespective of their socio-economic and religious identities and differences. Patriarchal notions of subordination, controlling the sexuality of woman and violence against her is justified and appreciated for restoring the lost honour.

No social stigma attaches to such honour crimes and there is no condemning of the perpetrators. Rather they are absolved of their guilt on the belief that sacrificing the natural bonds of love and kinship for preserving and restoring honour purifies the family.

It is always presumed justified to kill and die for honour (Omvedt, 1990:5-6), thereby compromising with the women's safety, choices and rights. There is a clear negation of her right to life, liberty, security and bodily integrity; sexual rights; rights to mobility, education, work and travel; freedom of expression, association and movement; right to prohibition on torture, cruel, inhuman and degrading treatment; right to freedom from gender based discrimination, sexual abuse and exploitation; right to privacy; right to marry and found a family; right to an effective remedy; right to equality before the Law, right to take decisions and right to self-development.

Global Legal Scenario Relating to Honour Crimes

The following tables specifically focus the existing legal and social scenario towards honour crimes in India, Jordan, Lebanon, Palestine, Pakistan, Egypt, Israel, Italy, Iraq and other countries (Welchman & Hossain, 2005; *http://en.wikipedia.org/wiki/Honour_killing)*

Table 3 Position in India.

Table 3
India

Legal Scenario	• There is no specific criminal law to deal with the offence of honour crimes. • Perpetrators of these crimes are tried under Section 300 of Indian Penal Code, 1860 which deals with murder. The punishment for murder is life imprisonment or capital punishment under Section 302 of Indian Penal Code, 1860. • Any killings motivated by grave and sudden provocation are viewed leniently. This provision may be used for reducing the punishment for the perpetrators of honour crimes.

Table 4 Position in Jordan.

Table 4
Jordan

About Honour Crimes	• Female relatives suspected of adultery, extramarital sexual relations or pregnancy outside marriage are targets. • Woman fearing honour crimes are confined in state prisons while the criminals are free outside. Jordan has one of the highest per-capita honour killing rates in the world. -United Nations Estimate (www.upiasia.com/Society_Culture).
Legal Scenario	• Article 340 of the Jordanian Penal Code excuses a man who kills or injures his wife or his female kin caught in the act of adultery & he may be punished with a light sentence not exceeding a year in prison. Article 340 is of mixed French, Turkish & Syrian origin & is derived from the Ottoman Penal Code, 1858 (Zuhur, p.25; *www.lotsofessays.com*). Article 340 provides that (1) *he who surprises his wife or one of his female mahrams "unlawfuls" committing adultery with another and kills, wounds or injures one or both of them, shall benefit from the exonerating or exempting excuse.* (2) *He who surprises his wife or one of his ascendants or descendants or siblings with another in an unlawful bed and kills or wounds or injures one or both of them shall benefit from the mitigating excuse.* • *Mahram* is a male relative like a brother, father, uncle or son & a *maharim* are the female relatives within the prohibited degrees (Zuhur, p.26). • Thus the first clause here exempts the perpetrator while the second clause mitigates the punishment. • Article 340 has been amended in 2001 & the amended provision replaces the excuse of exemption or exoneration with that of mitigation & extends the benefit of reduction of sentence to a woman who finds her husband committing adultery in the marital home. • But with change of government, this amendment was rejected.

Table 5 Position in Lebanon

Table 5
Lebanon

Family Structure	• Wife & children are property of the male head of family known as *rabb* denoting hierarchy, authority & ownership. • Father had right to kill his wife as he had right to kill his slave. • Woman has no dominant role except that of wife, mother or daughter & is allowed to do a job or pursue her studies for better marriage prospects.
About Honour	• Woman's body is a shameful thing *i.e., awra* & must be guarded by her family & society. Her body belongs to her father's family before marriage & to her husband & his family after marriage. • A woman having sexual intercourse with a man to whom she is not married is called *zina* & it is treated as a source of shame *i.e., ard* for the family members which tarnishes their honour *i.e., sharaf.*

	• Such relationship impugns honour of the female but not of the male partner without whose participation the crime would never occur & she has to face the consequences alone. • Only way to wipe away shame & restore the tarnished honour is to remove the thing causing it, *i.e.*, by killing the woman (almashriq.hiof.no; Zuhur, p. 14).
About Honour Crimes	• The victim is always a woman, related to the criminal by a blood tie up to the fourth degree. • Mother, daughter, sister, paternal niece, paternal or maternal cousin are the victims. She may be single, married, divorced or widowed. The perpetrator is mostly a man.
Legal Scenario	• *Article 562* of the Lebanon Penal Code provides scope for exempting the perpetrators of honour crimes & encourages men to commit such crimes. Lebanese Penal Code is influenced by the Ottoman & French penal laws. • *Before Amendment:* Article 562 provides that *whosoever surprises his spouse or one of his ascendants or descendants or his sister in a witnessed crime of adultery or in a situation of unlawful intercourse and proceeds to kill or injure one of them, without deliberation, shall benefit from the excuse of exemption. The person who kills or injures on surprising his spouse or his ascendants or descendants or his sister in a suspicious situation with another person shall benefit from the excuse of mitigation.**Those entitled to benefit are husband, ascendants, descendants, brother or half-brother. • After Lebanon has ratified the Convention on the Elimination of All Forms of Discrimination Against Women in 1996, due to efforts of the NGOs, Article 562 has been amended with effect from 10 February 1999. The amended version replaces the excuse of exemption in the first paragraph with the excuse of mitigation & deletes the second paragraph. • Article 193 stipulates that *if a judge finds out that the motive of a crime was honest, he shall be sentenced as follows: Life imprisonment instead of execution, imprisonment for life or for 15 years instead of life imprisonment with hard labor, temporary imprisonment instead of temporary imprisonment with hard labor or brief imprisonment instead of brief imprisonment with hard labor.'* Motive is defined by Article 192 as *the cause that possessed the doer to carry out the action or the final end he seeks.* These provisions empower the Judiciary to shower leniency upon the honour criminals.

Table 6 Position in Palestine.

Table 6
Palestine

About Honour	• Woman is expected to sacrifice her own personal needs, aspirations & desires for protecting family unity & honour. • Men use violence on woman for restoring their dominant status. • A man is expected to protect not only woman of his family but has to preserve the honour of all women in the society. Failure to protect shames the man. For protecting honour, woman &

	offending male can be killed & the punishment is cancelled if the woman & man agree to marry.
About Honour Crimes	• There are many techniques of silencing like female mutilation & femicide *i.e.*, killing for family honour. Femicide means the criminal act of taking the life of a female by a male relative for coping with the perceived *'ar' i.e.*, shame which her suspected behaviour has brought on the family. Killing buries the victim & also the disgrace associated with her. Women have to sacrifice their liberty, right to education & right of choosing their husband due to the fear of femicide.
Judicial approach	• Judiciary treats the offenders leniently on the ground that the real crime is committed by the woman by not being a *salima i.e.*, becoming damaged & the male perpetrator has merely acted to cleanse the shame & safeguard his honour. Courts have in many cases reduced the sentence of the killer & even justified his criminal act.

Table 7 Position in Pakistan

Table 7
Pakistan

About Honour	• The practice of honour killings is known as *kalakali* in southern Punjab; *karokari* in Sindh; *siyakari* in Balochistan & *taurtoora* in North West Frontier Province. • Practice of honour killings originated with the Baloch tribes of Balochistan & spread to the other communities.
About Honour Crimes	• Honour killings occur in all the four provinces of Pakistan & the tribal areas. • Usually women is killed by their brother, father, husband or son. • Pakistan has the highest number of "honour" killings per annum, believed to be between 800 and 1,000. - United Nations Estimate (*www.upiasia.com*).
Legal Scenario	• On 2 October 1990, three Ordinances were promulgated for amending Pakistan Penal Code. • The new law introduced different sentences for murder depending on the form of proof of murder & the relationship of the offender to the deceased without considering intensity of crime. This affected the treatment of honour crimes where the offender was usually related to the victim with almost no witnesses. • Offender can be sentenced to death only if he confesses or if the requisite number of credible eye-witnesses is available. In the absence of proof, only a sentence of life imprisonment can be passed. • Again, Section 306 (b) & (c) of Pakistan Penal Code exempt certain relatives from death sentence & life imprisonment. If the parents or grandparents murder their child or grandchild or when one murders one's spouse & there exists children from the marriage, they are exempted.

	• Section 307 provides that under certain situations death sentence shall not be applicable & sets no lower limit for sentencing. This provision gives ample scope for awarding light sentences for honour crimes. • Section 309 & 310 of PPC read with Section 345 of Cr.P.C permits the heirs of a murder victim or the victim of bodily hurt the right to forgive an accused or compromise with him in return for a compromise. As the perpetrators in honour crimes are usually the close relatives of the victim woman, chances of compromise between victim's heirs & murderer increases.
Judicial approach	• In *Ghulam Yaseen vs The State* (PLD 1994 Lahore 392), Lahore High Court held that a murder committed on account of *ghariat* is not the same as *qatl-e-amd i.e.*, deliberate murder & the persons found guilty deserve concession & five years sentence was awarded to the offender who had killed a man & his unmarried sister found in a compromising position. • In *Sardar Mohammad vs The State* (1997 MLD 3045), Lahore High Court declared that the offence committed on account of family honour is no offence & acquitted the father accused of murdering his daughter & her partner found in compromising position. • The trend is slowly changing. In *Muhammad Akram Khan vs The State* (PLD 2001 SC 96), Supreme Court of Pakistan held that nobody has any right to take the life of anybody in the name of *Ghairat* & honour killing amounts to murder simpliciter & violates the fundamental right to life & liberty guaranteed under Article 9 of the Constitution of Islamic Republic of Pakistan. However, here the defence failed to establish that the murder took place for engaging in immoral acts. • In *Muhammad Siddique vs The State* (PLD 2002 Lahore 444), the Lahore High Court confirmed the death sentence of the trial court despite a compromise between the parties. In this case, a man had killed his daughter, her husband & their child on the ground that the daughter had exercised her choice of marriage. The court held that murder in the name of honour is not merely the physical elimination of a man or woman but is a blow to the concept of a free, dynamic & egalitarian society. • In 2005, National Assembly of Pakistan passed a law to address honour crimes but it fails to check the above lacunas in the criminal law.

Table 8 Position in Egypt

Table 8
Egypt

About Honour	• Honour is associated with & represented by virginity & intact hymen of a woman. • Women are assumed to be virtuous by nature & any transgression in their conduct is violation of their femininity. But men are not considered virtuous by nature & their sexual excesses must be indulged. A fallen woman destroys herself, tarnishes the honour of her family & deserves to be killed.

	• Men's honour is measured by the sexual conduct of their family women. • Honour *i.e., sharaf* is known as *ard i.e.,* name & good reputation owned by the men of the family & is embodied in the sexual conduct of the women who is required to behave properly lest brings shame to the family. Woman who has reached puberty or is sexually active is presumed to be a danger & needs to be controlled by segregating her from the opposite sex. • Their behavior is controlled by female circumcision, preventing them from indulging in beneficial physical exercise as it may damage the hymen.
About Honour Crimes	• Girls with blocked hymen, bellies swollen with menstrual blood, girls having swelling stomach due to tumours, girls whose periods have stopped due to their anemic condition have been killed on suspicion of having lost their virginity.
Legal Scenario	• Article 237 of the Egyptian Penal Code, 1939 mitigates the husband intentionally murdering his wife guilty of adultery. It provides that *whosoever surprises his wife in the act of committing adultery and immediately kills her and the person committing adultery with her shall be punished with a prison sentence instead of serious punishments.* This provision reduces the sentence of a husband. • Article 17 of Egyptian Penal Code makes way for judicial discretion if there are mitigating circumstances for the perpetrator. This provision is invoked by the judiciary for excusing the perpetrators of honour crimes.

Table 9 Position in Israel

Table 9
Israel

About Honour	• Honour crimes are committed either in public or carried out in the family home & announced in the public by the offender to the village & rest of the family. By such announcement, offenders prove their ability to control their women's behaviour to the society & also deter other female family members from behaving in similar dishonourable way. • By announcing the crime in public, the honour lost due to victim's act stands regained. • Sometimes to avoid any legal action & punishment, crime is committed at a site away from the home & no public announcement is made.
About Honour Crimes	• Perpetrator is usually a brother, father, son, cousin, husband, father-in-law, paternal or maternal uncle, nephew or even sister & mother. • Crimes have been committed in most brutal manner like forcing the female member to take poison & if that does not work, to hang herself or to jump into the well & leaving her to die barring access to any medical help.
Legal Scenario	• Life sentence being penalty for murder under the Israeli Penal Law, 1997 can be mitigated by the Court if a severe mental

	disturbance limited the ability of the offender to understand what he was doing or how condemnable his deed was or to refrain from committing the deed or if the accused was in a state of extreme psychological distress caused by the deceased's act. 1995 Amendment to the Penal Law has included the above provision in the form of Article 300 (a). This provision is used by the Courts for mitigating the punishment in the case of honour crimes.

Table 10 Position in Italy

Table 10
Italy

About Honour	• A woman is honest if married, does not work, takes good care of her house & children. • A woman has a duty to preserve family honour by her passive conduct. She is considered inherently weak, men have the right & duty to protect them from their own weakness & the predatory intentions of other unrelated men. Fathers, brothers & husbands are bound to protect the family honour.
About Honour Crimes	• Woman committing adultery deprives her husband & her children of the moral support & values & thus deserves punishment. • Perpetrators of these crimes are male family members. • Female genital mutilation is common [Frattini, Franco (2010, September 23)].
Legal Scenario	• The Rocco Code protects the individual & sexual honour. • Article 587 of Rocco Code, 1931 provides that *any person discovering unlawful sexual relations i.e., sexual relations outside the marriage on the part of their spouse, daughter, sister and in the fit of fury occasioned by the offence to their family's honour causes their death shall be punished for a term from three to seven years.* A person killing the paramour is also subject to the same punishment. If in the above circumstance perpetrator causes personal injury, he will be subject to one third of the punishment of three months to three years prescribed for these offences under Article 582 & 583 of the Code. Thus the Code prescribes reduced punishment for honour crimes.

Table 11 Position in Iraq

Table 11
Iraq

Family structure	• Kurdish family is a socio-political organization consisting of extended family groups with common ancestors & living in the same household. Endogamy is an important rule requiring marriage inside the same extended family, clan & tribe & ensures male domination & is related to the honour-shame complex grounded in the theory of procreation. • Marriage is not an individual choice but a collective affair, arranged & imposed by the male members. For marriage outside the family or clan, a woman from the same territorial location is preferred.

About Honour	• Honour crimes are justified due to the victim's perceived or actual attitude or behaviour presumed to have dishonoured the family. Any behaviour breaching social or sexual norms violates family's honour. • There exists a council of elders in every tribe known as *rishspi* *i.e.*, white beards, exclusively made up of men who decide all the matters of honour violation & killings.
About Honour Crimes	• These crimes are publicly referred as purification of shame *i.e, ghasl al 'ar* & legally known as killings of women *i.e., qatl al nisaa.*
Legal Scenario	• Article 409 of the Iraqi Penal Code, 1969 provides that *any person who surprises his wife in the act of adultery or finds his girlfriend in bed with her lover and kills them immediately or one of them or assaults one of them so that he or she dies or is left permanently disabled is punishable by a period of detention not exceeding three years. It is not permissible to exercise the right of legal defence against any person who uses this excuse.* • Article 128 & 130-132 provide for mitigating the sentence & very light imprisonment. United Nations Special Rapporteur on Violence against Women reports that more than 4000 women have been victims of honour killings since the introduction of Article 128 in 1990 (UN Commission on Human Rights [January 2002]). • Amendment brought in 2002 provides that Article 128, 130 & 131 of the Iraqi Penal Code will not be implemented in crimes against women under the pretext of honourable motivation & the perpetrator shall not be benefitted of lenient punishment (Zuhur, p.29).
Judicial Opinion	• The Supreme Court has issued a decision in the Judicial Publication Journal of Baghdad stating that it is legally excused for anyone who commits murder for the purification of shame (*ghasl al-'ar*). • The courts have showed leniency on the ground of purification of shame, preservation of honour & cohesion of the family.

Table 12 Position in other countries

Table 12
Position in Other Countries

Bangladesh	• Concept of shame, *lojja* or *sharam* is invoked to prevent transgression of social norms. It is inculcated in the girls from their young age & is embodied in gestures, behaviour, movement & clothing. Lowered gaze, modest gait & silence are the indicia of positive shame. It is treated as immodest for a woman to discuss her marriage. A girl is socialized to believe that only her parents know what is best for her & only in exceptional cases they disagree to a marriage arranged by the parents. Subordination of a woman rests on the ability of the dominant social groups to regulate female sexuality (Welchman & Hossain, 2005:291).
Kuwait	• Reduced sentence of three years or less is prescribed for perpetrators of honour crimes (Zuhur, p. 26).
Tunisia	• A reduced sentence of five years is prescribed (Zuhur, p.26).

Syria	• Article 548 of the Syrian Penal Code exempts a man killing his wife, sister & other female family members committing adultery from penalty (Zuhur, p.27).
Uruguay	• Offence of murder of the spouse committed in the heat of passion caused by adultery is deemed fit for judicial pardon. Infidelity of partners & breaking up of relationship also mitigates the offence (Welchman & Hossain, 2005:247).
Honduras and Mexico	• A person killing his or her spouse or partner in the act of sexual intercourse with another person receives lighter sentence (Welchman & Hossain, 2005:247).
Ecuador	• Such offence is not treated as an offence at all (Welchman & Hossain, 2005:247).

Suggestions and Conclusion

Resolution 55/66 of the General Assembly was the first international document specifically addressing the issue of honour crimes by explicitly identifying such crimes as a human right issue. It clearly voices the obligation of State parties to exercise due diligence to prevent, investigate and punish the perpetrators of such crimes and provide protection to the victims.

Though the attitude of the community towards these crimes will change only gradually, need is there to adopt an approach equally coordinated on social and legal fronts. Some of the suggestions are specified below:

- There exists an immediate need to check the cruel culture of victimizing the female population for protecting and restoring the assumed notions of family and community honour.
- The penal codes providing for a reduced sentence or exemption to the perpetrators of honour crimes need an immediate reform.
- Any discretion provided to the Judiciary for showing leniency to the perpetrators of honour crimes should be taken away.
- Article 7 of the Constitution of Lebanon, Article 8 of the Constitution of Egypt, Article 6(a) of the Constitution of the Hashemite Kingdom of Jordan, Article 5 of the Constitution of Morocco, Article 25 of the Constitution of Syria, Article 19 of the Interim Constitution of Iraq, 1990, Article 25 of the Constitution of Pakistan, Article of 14 of the Constitution of India confer equality before law and equal protection of law to all irrespective of sex. These provisions ought to be implemented in spirit.
- Though majority of the International Conventions, Declarations and Protocols confer the right to marry and found a family on a woman; assure her freedom from arbitrary interference with privacy, family, home; assure her equality of treatment on par with men; prohibit discrimination and prejudice against her; prescribe elimination of all forms of violence against her; treat violence against her as a serious

offence, nations have failed in their endeavour to protect her rights due to their lack of motivation in this direction. States should be held legally liable for the honour killings since they have failed to protect the interest of their female population.

- It has to be borne in mind that violence in any form against woman totally nullifies her enjoyment of basic human rights and constitutes violation of the international treaties.
- Non-governmental organizations should be motivated to create awareness among the community members regarding the seriousness of the honour crimes.
- Insensitivity and gender bias prevalent among the judicial officers results in injustice to the victims of honour crimes. Such bias should be minimized.
- Need is there to make proper use of the forces within a community for combating the honour crimes. Media, newspapers, public debates and discussions in different public forums across the country, formal and informal education in schools and in towns, cities and villages for making the people aware about the cruelty of these crimes.
- There exists a need to transform the family and community attitude towards these crimes by having a discourse with them as no strategy to combat and check the crimes relating to honour can be successful without their consent and cooperation.
- There exists an immense need of gender sensitization programs for the judiciary, elders in the society, parents, young men, police and law makers.
- Need is there to spread the message of Manusmriti throughout the world. Manu prescribes highest respect, regard and protection for the women throughout their life. Woman must be honoured by the male members of her family (Manusmriti.III.55 -Jois, 2002:30; Buhler, 1990:85) as the gods are pleased but if dishonoured no sacred rites yield any rewards (Manusmriti.III.56 -Jois, 2002:30; Buhler, 1990:85) and the family perishes (Manusmriti.III.57, 58 -Jois, 2002:30-31; Buhler, 1990:85).
- Spirit of Common brotherhood as prescribed by Vedas ought to be diffused (Rigveda, Mandala 5, Sukta 60, Mantra 5 -Jois, 2002:xii).

The preciousness of human life over the family honour needs to be instilled in the minds of men before it is too late.

References

Banerjee-Dube, Ishita. (Ed.) (2008), *Caste in History*. New Delhi: Oxford University Press.

Brutal Justice: Pak Woman loses nose, hair to extramarital affair. (November 30, 2010). *Deccan Herald*, p. 13.

Buhler, G. (1990), *The Laws of Manu*. New Delhi: Ahuja Book Company.

Chakravarti, Uma (2003), *Gendering Caste: Through a Feminist Lens*. Calcutta: Stree.

Chaudhry, D.R. (2010, August 1), Feudal Mindset: In the heart of darkness. *Deccan Herald*, p. 1.

Chowdhary, Prem (2007), *Contentious Marriages, Eloping Couples: Gender, Caste and Patriarchy in Northern India*. New Delhi: Oxford University Press.

Dewan, V. K. (2000), *Law Relating to Offences Against Women*. New Delhi: Orient Law House.

Edwards, Susan (Ed.) (1985), *Gender, Sex and the Law*. London: Croom Helm.

Honour Killing. Retrieved August 27, 2010, from *http://en.wikipedia.org/wiki/Honour_killing visited on August 27, 2010 at 10.44 am.*

http://www.upiasia.com/Society_Culture/2008/04/07/an_appeal_to_jordan_to_stop_honor_killings/1109/ visited on February 19, 2011 at 11.39 am.

*http://www.lotsofessays.com/*viewpaper/1700492.html visited on February 19, 2011 at 11.27 am.

http://almashriq.hiof.no/lebanon/300/390/392/getting-away.html visited on February 19, 2011 at 11.48 am.

Jois, M. Rama (2002), *Ancient Indian Law- Eternal Values in Manu Smriti*. Delhi, Universal Publishing Co.

Omvedt, Gail (1990), *Violence Against Women: New Movements and New Theories in India*. New Delhi: Kali for Women.

Pandey, Sanjay (2010, July 20), Girl pays with her life for marrying Dalit. *Deccan Herald*, p. 13.

Pandey, Sanjay (2010, November 15), Talking Tough: Khap Panchayats refuse to mend medieval ways. *Deccan Herald*, p. 8.

UN Commission on Human Rights, "Report of the Special Rapporteur on Violence against Women" [January 2002].

Welchman, Lynn., & Hossain, Sara. (Ed.) (2005), *Honour*. Victoria: Spinifex Press & London: Zed Books.

Zuhur, Sherifa. *Gender, Sexuality and the criminal laws in the Middle East and North Africa: A Comparative Study*, retrieved from.

www.wwhr.org visited on February 19, 2011 at 12.54 pm.

DOMESTIC VIOLENCE AGAINST WOMEN: A HUMAN RIGHTS VIOLATION

*B. Suguna Reddy**

Introduction

Violence against women and girls continues to be a global epidemic that kills, tortures, and maims-physically, psychologically, sexually and economically. It is one of the most pervasive of human rights violations, denying women and girls equality, security, dignity, self-worth and their right to enjoy fundamental freedoms. Violence against women is present in every country cutting across boundaries of culture, class, education, income, ethnicity and age. Even though most societies prescribe violence against women, the reality is that violations against women's human rights are often sanctioned under the garb of cultural practices and norms, or through misinterpretation of religious tenets. Moreover, when the violation takes place within the home, as is very often the case, the abuse is effectively condoned by the tacit silence and the passivity displayed by the state and the law-enforcing machinery. The global dimensions of this violence are alarming, as highlighted by studies on its incidence and prevalence. No society can claim to be free of such violence, the only variation is in the patterns and trends that exist in countries and regions. Specific groups of women are more vulnerable, including minority groups, indigenous and migrant women, refugee women and those in situations of armed conflict, women in institutions and detention, women with disabilities, female children, and elderly women.

The term "domestic violence" includes violence against women and girls by an intimate partner, including a cohabiting partner, and by other family members, whether this violence

---

* *Professor, Former Registrar, Dept. of Women's Studies, Sri Padmavati Mahila Visva Vidyalayam, Tirupati–517 502.*

occurs within or beyond the confines of the home. In other words, the term "domestic" refers to the types of relationships involved rather than the place where the violent act occurs. It emphasizes the need for coordinated and integrated policy responses; enhancing partnerships between stakeholders; setting up mechanisms for monitoring and evaluating programmes and policies; implementing existing legislation; and ensuring greater transparency and accountability from governments in order to eliminate violence against women and girls. Women's groups have long pushed for such responses, and have placed women's rights firmly on the agenda of international human rights through their advocacy. The 1990s, in particular, witnessed concentrated efforts on the part of the world community to legitimize and mainstream the issue. The World Conference on Human Rights in Vienna (1993) accepted that the rights of women and girls are "an inalienable, integral and indivisible part of universal human rights." The United Nations General Assembly in December 1993, adopted the Declaration on the Elimination of Violence against Women. It is the first international human rights instrument to deal exclusively with violence against women, a groundbreaking document that became the basis for many other parallel process.

In 1994, the Commission on Human Rights appointed the first UN Special Rapporteur on Violence against Women, entrusting her with the task of analyzing and documenting the phenomenon and holding governments accountable for violation against women. The Fourth World Conference on Women in Beijing (1995) included elimination of all forms of violence against women as one of its twelve strategic objectives, and listed concrete actions to be taken by the governments, the United Nations, international and non-governmental organizations. While gender-based violence is not specifically mentioned in the 1979 Convention on the Elimination of All Forms of Discrimination against Women (CEDAW), in 1992 the Committee over-seeing CEDAW implementation adopted General Recommendation 19, which states that it is a form of discrimination that inhibits a woman's ability to enjoy rights and freedoms on a basis of equality with men. It asks that governments take this into consideration when reviewing their laws and policies.

The family is often equated with sanctuary - a place where individuals seek love, safety, security and shelter. But the evidence shows that it is also a place that imperils lives and breeds some of the most drastic forms of violence perpetrated against women and girls. Violence in the domestic sphere is usually perpetrated by males who are, or who have been, in positions of trust and intimacy and power – husbands, fathers, fathers-in-laws, stepfathers, brothers, uncles, sons or other relatives. Domestic violence is in most cases violence perpetrated by men against women. Women can also be violent, but their actions account for a small percentage of domestic violence.

Table 1
Types of Violence Against Women

Phase	*Type of violence*
Pre-birth	Sex-selective abortion; effects of battering during pregnancy on birth outcomes.
Infancy	Female infanticide; physical, sexual and psychological abuse.
Girlhood	Child marriage; female genital mutilation, physical, sexual and psychological abuse, child prostitution and pornography.
Adolescence and Adulthood	Dating and courtship violence (e.g. acid throwing and date rape) economically coerced sex (e.g. school girls having sex with "sugar daddies" in return for school fees), sexual abuse in the workplace, rape, sexual harassment, forced prostitution and pornography, trafficking in women; partner violence, marital rape, dowry abuse and murders, partner homicide, psychological abuse, abuse of women with disabilities, forced pregnancy.
Elderly	Forced "suicide" or homicide of widows for economic reasons, sexual, physical and psychological abuse.

Source: "Violence Against Women", WHO., FRH/WHD/97.8

Violence against women is often a cycle of abuse that manifests itself in many forms throughout their lives. Even at the very beginning of her life, a girl may be the target of sex-selective abortion or female infanticide in cultures where son preference is prevalent. During childhood, violence against girls may include enforced malnutrition, lack of access to medical care and education, incest, female genital mutilation, early marriage and forced prostitution or bonded labour. Some go on to suffer throughout their adult lives battered, raped and even murdered at the hands of intimate partners. Other crimes of violence against women include forced pregnancy, abortion or sterilization and harmful traditional practices such as dowry related violence, sati (the burning of a widow on the funeral pyre of her husband), and killing in the name of honour. And in later life, widows and elderly women may also experience abuse. While the impact of physical abuse may be more 'visible' than psychological scarring, repeated humiliation and insults, forced isolation, limitations on social mobility, constant threats of violence and injury and denial of economic resources are more subtle and insidious forms of violence. The intangible nature of psychological abuse makes it harder to define and report, leaving the woman in a situation where she is often made to feel mentally destabilized and powerless. Jurists and human rights experts and activists have argued that the physical, sexual and psychological abuse sometimes with fatal outcomes, inflicted on women is comparable to torture in both its nature and severity. It can be perpetrated intentionally, and committed for the specific purposes of punishment, intimidation, and control of the woman's identity and behaviour. It makes place in situations where a woman may seen free to leave, but is held prisoner by fear of further violence against herself and her children or by lack of resources, family, legal or community support.

Magnitude of the Problem

The extent, validity and reliability of the data available are critical in determining the magnitude of the problem and in identifying priority areas for intervention. Prevalence studies with samples of representative populations are relatively new in developing countries. Such studies were initially conducted in industrialized countries the United States, Canada, and Europe. For example, one very influential survey conducted in Canada in 1993 under the auspices of the Canadian government was developed in consultation with women's organizations and ensured adequate support and services for women participating in the survey. Some countries have begun to legislate against marital rape. These include Australia, Austria, Barbados, Canada, Cyprus, Denmark, the Dominican Republic, Ecuador, Finland, France, Germany, Ireland, Mexico, Namibia, New Zealand, Norway, the Philippines, Poland, Russia, South Africa, Spain, Sweden, Trinidad & Tobago, the United Kingdom and the United States of America. Although provision of such laws represents considerable progress, it is often difficult for a woman to press charges because of the evidential rules concerning the crime. The following table shows the prevalence of Domestic Violence against women in other countries:

Table 2
Domestic Violence against Women

Industrialized Countries
Canada
• 29% of women (a nationally representative sample of 12,300 women) reported being physically assaulted by a current or former partner since the age of 16.
Japan
• 59% of 796 women surveyed in 1993 reported being physically abused by their partner.
New Zealand
• 20% of 314 women surveyed reported being hit or physically abused by a male partner.
Switzerland
• 1,500 women reported being physically assaulted according to a 1997 survey.
United Kingdom
• 25% of women (a random sample of women from one district) had been punched or slapped by a partner or ex-partner in their lifetime.
United States
• 28% of women (a nationally representative sample of women) reported at lease one episode of physical violence from their partner.
Asia and the Pacific
Cambodia
• 16% of women (a nationally representative sample of women) reported being physically abused by a spouse; 8% report being injured.

Contd...

India

- Upto 45% of married men acknowledged physically abusing their wives, according to a 1996 survey of 6,902 men in the state of Uttar Pradesh.

Korea

- 38% of wives reported being physically abused by their spouse, based on a survey of a random sample of women.

Thailand

- 20% of husbands (a representative sample of 619 husbands) acknowledged physically abusing their wives at least once in their marriage.

Middle East

Egypt

- 35% of women (a nationally representative sample of women) reported being beaten by their husband at some point in their marriage.

Israel

- 32% of women reported at least one episode of physical abuse by their partner and 30% report sexual coercion by their husbands in the previous year, according to a 1997 survey of 1,826 Arab Women.

Africa

Kenya

- 42% of 612 women surveyed in one district reported having been beaten by a partner; of those 58% reported that they were beaten often or sometimes.

Uganda

- 41% of women reported being beaten or physically harmed by a partner; 41% of men reported beating their partner (representative sample of women and their partners in two districts)

Zimbabwe

- 32% of 966 women in one province reported physical abuse by a family or household member since the age of 16, according to a 1996 survey.

Latin America and the Caribbean

Chile

- 26% of women (representative sample of women from Santiago) reported at least one episode of violence by a partner, 11% reported at least one episode of severe violence and 15% of women reported at least one episode of less severe violence.

Colombia

- 19% of 6,097 women surveyed have been physically assaulted by their partner in their lifetime.

Mexico

- 30% of 650 women surveyed in Guadalajara reported at least one episode of physical violence by a partner; 13% reported physical violence within the previous year, according to a 1997 report.

Nicaragua

- 52% of women (representative sample of women in Leon) reported being physically abused by a partner at least.

Contd...

Central and Eastern Europe/CIS/Baltic States

Estonia

- 29% of women aged 18-24 fear domestic violence, and the share rises with age, affecting 52% of women 65 or older, according to a 1994 survey of 2,315 women.

Poland

- 60% of divorced women surveyed in 1993 by the Centre for the Examination of Public Opinion reported having been hit at least once by their ex-husbands; an additional 25% reported repeated violence.

Russia (St. Petersburg)

- 25% of girls (and 11% of boys) reported unwanted sexual contact, according to a survey of 174 boys and 172 girls in grade 10 (aged 14-17).

Tajikistan

- 23% of 550 women aged 18-40 reported physical abuse, according to a survey.

Source: "Violence Against Women,"WHO, FRH/WHD/97.8, "Women in Transition, "Regional Monitoring Report, UNICEF 1999, and a study by Domestic Violence Research Centre, Japan.)

Causes of Domestic Violence

There is no one single factor to account for violence perpetrated against women. Increasingly, research has focused on the inter-relatedness of various factors that should improve the understanding of the problem within different cultural contexts.

Several complex and interconnected institutionalized social and cultural factors have kept women particularly vulnerable to the violence directed at them, all of those manifestations are historically unequal power relations between men and women. Factors contributing to these unequal power relations include: socio-economic forces, the family institution where power relations are enforced, fear of and control over female sexuality, belief in the inherent superiority of males and legislation and cultural sanctions that have traditionally denied women and children an independent legal and social status. Lack of economic resources underpins women's vulnerability to violence and their difficulty in extricating themselves from a violent relationship. The link between violence and lack of economic resources and dependence is circular. On the one hand, the threat and fear of violence keeps women from seeking employment, or at best compels them to accept low-paid, home based exploitative labour. And on the other, without economic independence. Women have no power to escape from an abusive relationship.

Experiences during childhood, such as witnessing domestic violence and experiencing physical and sexual abuse, have been identified as factors that put children at risk. Violence may be learnt as a means of resolving conflict and asserting manhood by children who have witnessed such patterns of conflict resolution. Excessive consumption of alcohol and other drugs has also been noted as a factor in provoking aggressive and violent male behaviour towards women and children. A survey of domestic violence in Moscow revealed that

Table 3

Factors That Perpetuate Domestic Violence

Cultural	• Gender specific socialization • Cultural definitions of appropriate sex roles • Expectations of roles within relationships • Belief in the inherent superiority of males. • Values that give men proprietary rights over women and girls • Notion of the family as the private sphere and under male control • Customs of marriage (bride price/dowry) • Acceptability of violence as a means to resolve conflict.
Economic	• Women's economic dependence on men • Limited access to cash and credit • Discriminatory laws regarding inheritance, property rights, use of communal lands and maintenance after divorce or widowhood • Limited access to employment in formal and informal sectors • Limited access to education and training for women
Legal	• Lesser legal status of women either by written law and/or by practice • Laws regarding divorce, child custody, maintenance and inheritance • Legal definitions of rape and domestic abuse • Low levels of legal literacy among women • Insensitive treatment of women and girls by police and judiciary.
Political	• Under representation of women in power, politics, the media and in the legal and medical professions. • Domestic violence not taken seriously • Notions of family being private and beyond control of the state • Risk of challenge to status quo/religious laws • Limited organizations of women as a political force • Limited participation of women in organized political system

Source: Heise. 1994

half the cases of physical abuse are associated with the husband's excessive alcohol consumption.

Lack of legal protection, particularly within the sanctity of the home, is a strong factor in perpetuating violence against women. Until recently, the public/private distinction that has ruled most legal systems has been a major obstacle to women's rights. Increasingly, however, States are seen as responsible for protecting the rights of women even in connection with offences committed within the home. In many countries violence against women is exacerbated by legislation, law enforcement and judicial systems that do not recognize domestic violence as a crime. The challenge is to end impunity for the perpetrators as one means of preventing future abuse.

Consequences

Denial of Fundamental Rights

Perhaps the most crucial consequence of violence against women and girls is the denial of fundamental human rights to women and girls. International human rights instruments such as the Universal Declaration of Human Rights (UDHR) adopted in 1948, the Convention on the Elimination of All Forms of Discrimination Against Women (CEDAW) adopted in 1979 and the Convention on the Rights of the Child (CRC) adopted in 1989 affirm the principle of fundamental rights and freedoms of every human being. Both CEDAW and the CRC are guided by a broad concept of human rights that stretches beyond civil and political rights to the core issues of economic survival, health, and education that affect the quality of daily life for most women and children. The two Conventions call for the right to protection from gender-based abuse and neglect. The strength of these treaties rests on an international consensus and the assumption that all practices that harm women and girls no matter how deeply they are embedded in culture must be eradicated. Legally binding under international law for governments that have ratified them, these treaties oblige governments not only to protect women from crimes of violence, but also to investigate violations when they occur and to bring the perpetrators to justice.

Human Development Goals Undermined

There is a growing recognition that countries cannot reach their full potential as long as women's potential to participate fully in their society is denied. Data on the social, economic and health costs of violence leave no doubt that violence against women undermines progress towards human and economic development. Women's participation has become key in all social development programmes, be they environmental, for poverty alleviation, or for good governance. By hampering the full involvement and participation of women, countries are eroding the human capital of half their populations. True indicators of a country's commitment to gender equality lie in its action to eliminate violence against women in all its forms and in all areas of life.

Health Consequences

Domestic violence against women leads to far reaching physical and psychological consequences, some with fatal outcomes.

Impact on Children

Children who have witnessed domestic violence or have themselves been abused, exhibit health and behaviour problems, including problems with their weight, their eating, and their sleep. They may have difficulty at school and find it hard to develop close and positive friendships. They may try to run away or even display suicidal tendencies.

Domestic Violence and HIV/AIDS

Nearly 14 million women today are infected with HIV and the rate of female infection is rising. A forthcoming study from WHO finds that the greatest risk of HIV infection for many women comes from a regular partner, and is

Table 4

Health Consequences of Violence Against Women

Non-Fatal Outcomes Physical health outcomes

- Injury (from lacerations to fractures and internal organs injury)
- Unwanted pregnancy
- Gynaecological problems
- STDs including HIV/AIDS
- Miscarriage
- Pelvic inflammatory disease
- Chronic Pelvic pain
- Headaches
- Permanent disabilities
- Asthama
- Irritable bowel syndrome
- Self-injurious behavious (smoking, unprotected sex)

Mental health outcomes

- Depression
- Fear
- Anxiety
- Low self-esteem
- Sexual dysfunction
- Eating problems
- Obsessive-compulsive disorder
- Post traumatic stress disorder

Fatal Out Comes

- Suicide
- Homicide
- Maternal mortality
- HIV/AIDS

Source: "Violence against Women", WHO Consultation, 1996

heightened by an unequal relationship that makes it difficult, if not impossible, to negotiate safe sex. For these women, sex is not a matter of choice.

A study of women aged 18 and over in one province in Zimbabwe found that 26 per cent of married women reported being forced to have sex when they did not want to. It is widely acknowledged that, even when a woman is aware that her partner has other sexual partners, or is HIV infected, she may not be in a position to insist on condom use or monogamy. Most HIV/AIDS prevention programmes, however, advocate both methods. Many women would feel that any attempt to discuss such measures would provoke yet more violence.

Other studies have found that the spread of HIV/AIDS in some parts of Africa is being exacerbated by practices that see women as the 'property' of men. The tradition of wife of widow inheritance, for example, is faily common in eastern and southern Africa. When a woman's husband dies, his wife and property are often inherited by his eldest brother. In western Kenya women have been forced to marry, even when their husbands have died of AIDS, when they themselves are infected, or when their future husband has AIDS. There are no laws to address this practice in Kenya.

Sexual cleansing is a more recent phenomena, resulting from, and contributing to the spread of HIV/AIDS. Practised within extended families in western Kenya, Zimbabwe and parts of Ghana, it is based on the belief that a man can be cured of HIV/AIDS if he has sex with a young girl who is a virgin. Girls as young as eight are selected to ensure their purity.

A new approach is required that acknowledges the links between violence against women and the spread of HIV/AIDS, and translates this into policies and programmes for HIV prevention and care.

Combating Domestic Violence: Obligations of the State

Domestic violence, whether it is perpetrated by private or state actors, constitutes a violation of human rights. It is the duty of states to ensure that there is no impunity for the perpetrators of such violence. Often state policies and inaction perpetuate or condone such violence within the domestic sphere. States have a double duty under international human rights law. They are not only required not to commit human rights violations, but also to prevent and respond to human rights abuses. In the past, human rights protection was interpreted narrowly state inaction to prevent and punish violations was not viewed as a failure in its duty to protect human rights. The concept of state responsibility has now develop to recognize that states also have an obligation to take preventive and punitive steps where rights violations by private actors occur.

International Legal Standards

Three doctrines, developed by human rights scholars and activists, have to be taken into account when dealing with the issue of violence against women by private actors. The first is that states have a responsibility to exercise due diligence to prevent, investigate and punish international law violations and pay just compensation.

Domestic Violence as Torture

Domestic violence is a form of torture and should be dealt with accordingly. The argument is that, depending on the severity and the circumstances giving rise to state responsibility, domestic violence can constitute torture or cruel, inhuman and degrading treatment or punishment under the International Covenant on Civil and Political Rights, and the Convention Against Torture and Other Cruel, inhuman or degrading treatment or punishment.

It is argued that domestic violence involves the very four critical elements that constitute torture: (a) it causes severe physical and or mental pain, it is (b) intentionally inflicted, (c) for specified purposes and (d) with some form of official involvement, whether active or passive.

Responses to Combat Domestic Violence

Today, many States recognize the importance of protecting women from abuse and punishing the perpetrators of the crimes. One of the major questions facing law reformers is whether to *'criminalize'* wife battery. There is a sense that domestic violence is a crime between those who are linked by bonds of intimacy.

Criminalization

Advocates of the criminal justice approach point to the symbolic power of the law and argue that arrest, prosecution and conviction, with punishment, is a process that carries the clear condemnation of society for the conduct of the abuser and acknowledges his personal responsibility for the activity.

Legislation

Legislation with regard to domestic violence is a modern phenomenon. There is an increasing belief that special laws should be drafter having special remedies and procedures. The first problem that arises with regard to legislation is to allow for prosecution of men who beat their spouses even if the latter under pressure want to withdraw their claims. In response some countries have instructed police and prosecutors to proceed with cases even in situations where women indicated that they would rather not proceed.

Police Action

In most jurisdictions the power of the police to enter private premised is limited. In the context of domestic violence this can protect the violent man at the expense of the woman. Some legislations allow the police to enter if requested to do so by a person who apparently resides on the premises or where the officer has reason to believe that a person on the premises is under attack or imminent attack. In many cases of domestic violence, immediate release of the offender on bail may be dangerous for the woman and, certainly release without prior warning may have serious consequences for her.

Training and Community Support Services

Most police, prosecutors, magistrates, judges and doctors adhere to traditional values that support the family as an institution and the dominance of the male party within it. Therefore it is necessary to train law enforcers and medical and legal professionals who come in contact with those experiencing violence to understand gender violence to appreciate the trauma of those suffering and to take proper evidence for criminal proceedings.

Conclusion

Overwhelmingly, governments lack the necessary expertise to develop and implement policy relating to violence against women. Therefore, a more cooperative relationship between governments and civil society should be built to combat violence against women. An integrated, multidisciplinary approach with lawyers, psychologists, social workers, doctors and others working together to gain a holistic understanding of each particular case and the needs of the individual is the best option. Giving attention to the real life context of the battered woman, her hopelessness, dependency, restricted options, and her consequent need for empowerment, should underpin every approach. The goal is to work with her to develop her capacity to decide her own future.

References

Gail Omvedt (1990), Violence Against Women, New Movements and New Theories in Inaid, Kali Primaries, New Delhi.

Suguna Reddy B. (2000), Structural Violence Against Women, *Journal of Social Welfare*, Vol. 47, No. 9.

Shimin Kudchedkar and Sabiha Al-Issa (elditors), (1998), Violence Against Women, Peneraft Internations, New Delhi.

UNDP (2000), Human Development Report, Oxford University Press.

Vidya Shah and Devika Sahdev (2004), Strength in Action: An Education Guide to Preventing Domestic Violence, Break Through, New Delhi.

CHILD ABUSE

A. Vinayagamoorthy, R. C. Padmapriya** & C. Gayathiri***

Introduction

"Child abuse" can be defined as causing or permitting any harmful or offensive contact on a child's body; and, any communication or transaction of any kind which humiliates, shames, or frightens the child. Some child development experts go a bit further, and define child abuse as any act or omission, which fails to nurture or in the upbringing of children. A child of any age, sex, race, religion, and socioeconomic background can fall victim to child abuse and neglect.

There are many factors that may contribute to the occurrence of child abuse and neglect. Parents who abuse drugs or alcohol may be more likely to maltreat their children. Some parents may not be able to cope with the stress resulting from the changes and may experience difficulty in caring for their children.

Legal Definitions

The Federal Child Abuse Prevention and Treatment Act (CAPTA) provides minimum standards for definitions. CAPTA states,

> "The term 'child abuse and neglect' means, at a minimum, any recent act or failure to act on the part of a parent or caretaker, which results in death, serious physical or emotional harm, sexual abuse or exploitation, or an act or failure to act which presents an imminent risk of serious harm".

---

* *Assistant Professor, Department of Commerce, Periyar University, Salem–636 0 11 Tamilnadu.*

** *M. Phil., Research Scholar, Department of Commerce, Periyar University, Salem–636011, Tamilnadu.*

Basic Concepts

Child abuse has serious physical and psycho-social consequences which adversely affect the health and overall well-being of a child. According to WHO: "Child abuse or maltreatment constitutes all forms of physical and/or emotional ill-treatment, sexual abuse, neglect or negligent treatment or commercial or other exploitation, resulting in actual or potential harm to the child's health, survival, development or dignity in the context of a relationship of responsibility, trust or power."

Child abuse is a violation of the basic human rights of a child and is an outcome of a set of inter-related familial, social, psychological and economic factors. The problem of child abuse and human rights violation is one of the most critical matters on the international human rights agenda.

Scope and Importance

Child abuse contributes to teen prostitution. More than 95% of teenage prostitutes have been sexually abused. Furthermore, teenage prostitution leads to drugs, abuse and other serious crimes.

Long term effects of child abuse include fear, anxiety, depression, anger, hostility, inappropriate sexual behavior, poor self esteem, tendency toward substance abuse and difficulty with close relationships. This has a huge impact on the Society.

The average cost for treatment of alcohol or drug abuse in outpatient facilities was an estimated $1,433 per course of treatment according to a report released by The Substance Abuse and Mental Health Services Administration (SAMHSA).

The effect of child abuse on our society is overwhelming and getting worse. Many victims of child abuse will also abuse their own children, which is why child abuse has risen to such an unbelievable level.

There is a well-documented link between childhood abuse and long-term health effects. These long-term effects can include increased risk of teen pregnancy or sexually transmitted disease, central nervous system damage, speech problems, inhibited growth, mental and emotional disturbances, delayed language development, low self-esteem, and aggressive tendencies (Chalk, Gibbons, and Scarupa, 2002; Kelley, Thornberry, and Smith, 1997).

Major Types of Abuse

- Emotional Abuse
- Neglect
- Physical Abuse
- Sexual Abuse.

Emotional Abuse

Emotional abuse known as verbal abuse, mental abuse, and psychological maltreatment includes acts or the failures to act by parents or caretakers that have caused or could cause serious behavioral, cognitive, emotional, or mental disorders. This can include parents/caretakers using extreme and/or bizarre forms of punishment, such as confinement in a closet or dark room or being tied to a chair for long periods of time or threatening or terrorizing a child. Less severe acts, but no less damaging are belittling or rejecting treatment, using derogatory terms to describe the child, habitual scapegoating or blaming.

Neglect

Neglect is the failure to provide for the child's basic needs. Neglect can be physical, educational, or emotional. Physical neglect can include not providing adequate food or clothing, appropriate medical care, supervision, or proper weather protection. It may include abandonment. Educational neglect includes failure to provide appropriate schooling or special educational needs, allowing excessive truancies. Psychological neglect includes the lack of any emotional support and love, never attending to the child, spousal abuse, drug and alcohol abuse including allowing the child to participate in drug and alcohol use.

Physical Abuse

Physical abuse is inflicting of physical injury upon a child. This may include, burning, hitting, punching, shaking, kicking, beating, or otherwise harming a child. The parent/caretaker may not have intended to hurt the child, the injury is not an accident. It may, however, be the result of over-discipline or physical punishment that is inappropriate to the child's age.

Sexual Abuse

Sexual abuse is the inappropriate sexual behavior with a child. It includes fondling a child's genitals, making the child fondle the adult's genitals, intercourse, incest, rape, sodomy, exhibitionism and sexual exploitation. To be considered child abuse these acts have to be committed by a person responsible for the care of a child or related to the child. If a stranger commits these acts, it would be considered sexual assault and handled solely be the police and criminal courts.

Commercial or other exploitation of a child refers to use of the child in work or other activities for the benefits of others. This includes, but is not limited to, child labour and child prostitution. These activities are to the detriment of the child's physical or mental health, education, or spiritual, moral or social-emotional development.

Consequences

The consequences are as follows.

1. It will encourage the child to lie, resent, fear, and retaliate, instead of loving, trusting, and listening.
2. It will alilenate the child from the parents and the rest of the family and make him a recluse.
3. It will lower the child's self esteem, and affects the child's psychological development and ability to behave normally outside his home.
4. When the child grow up, it could probably carry on the family tradition, and abuse the grandchildren.
5. The child may exclude the parents in his adult life.

Fatalities

A child abuse fatality is when a child's death is the result of abuse or neglect, or when abuse and/or neglect are contributing factors to a child's death. In the India, 1,730 children died in 2008 due to factors related to abuse; this is a rate of 2.33 per 100,000 Indian children. Child abuse fatalities are widely recognized as being under-counted; it is estimated that between 60-85% of child fatalities due to maltreatment are not recorded as such on death certificates.

Younger children are at a much higher risk of being killed. Girls and boys, however, are killed at similar rates. Caregivers, and specifically mothers, are more likely to be the perpetrators of a child abuse fatality, than anyone else, including strangers, relatives, and non-relative caregivers. Family situations which place children at risk include moving, unemployment, having non-family members living in the household.

A number of policies and programs have been put into place to try to better understand and to prevent child abuse fatalities, including: safe haven laws, child fatality review teams, training for investigators, shaken baby syndrome prevention programs, and child abuse death laws which mandate harsher sentencing for taking the life of a child.

Causes

Child abuse is a complex phenomenon with multiple causes. Understanding the causes of abuse is crucial to addressing the problem of child abuse. Parents who physically abuse their spouses are more likely than others to physically abuse their children. However, it is impossible to know whether marital strife is a cause of child abuse, or if both the marital strife and the abuse are caused by tendencies in the abuser.

Substance abuse can be a major contributing factor to child abuse. One U.S. study found that parents with documented substance abuse, most commonly alcohol, cocaine, and heroin, were much more likely to mistreat their children, and were also much more likely to reject court-ordered services and treatments.

Unemployment and financial difficulties are associated with increased rates of child abuse. In 2009 CBS News reported that child abuse in the United States had increased during the economic recession. It gave the example of a father who had never been the primary care-taker of the children. Now that the father was in that role, the children began to come in with injuries.

Effects

Children with a history of neglect or physical abuse are at risk of developing psychiatric problems, or a disorganized attachment style. Disorganized attachment is associated with a number of developmental problems, including dissociative symptoms, as well as anxiety, depressive, and acting out symptoms. A study by Dante Cicchetti found that 80% of abused and maltreated infants exhibited symptoms of disorganized attachment. When some of these children become parents, especially if they suffer from posttraumatic stress disorder (PTSD), dissociative symptoms, and other sequelae of child abuse, they may encounter difficulty when faced with their infant and young children's needs and normative distress, which may in turn lead to adverse consequences for their child's social-emotional development.

Victims of childhood abuse, it is claimed, also suffer from different types of physical health problems later in life. Some reportedly suffer from some type of chronic head, abdominal, pelvic, or muscular pain with no identifiable reason. Even though the majority of childhood abuse victims know or believe that their abuse is, or can be, the cause of different health problems in their adult life, for the great majority their abuse was not directly associated with those problems, indicating that sufferers were most likely diagnosed with other possible causes for their health problems, instead of their childhood abuse.

The effects of child abuse vary, depending on the type of abuse. A 2006 study found that childhood emotional and sexual abuse were strongly related to adult depressive symptoms, while exposure to verbal abuse and witnessing of had a moderately strong association, and physical abuse a moderate one. For depression, experiencing more than two kinds of abuse exerted synergetically stronger symptoms. Sexual abuse was particularly deleterious in its intrafamilial form, for symptoms of depression, anxiety, dissociation, and limbic irritability Childhood verbal abuse had a stronger association with anger-hostility than any other type of abuse studied, and was second only to emotional abuse in its relationship with dissociative symptoms.

Physical Health Consequences

The immediate physical effects of abuse or neglect can be relatively minor or severe. In some cases the physical effects are temporary; however, the pain and suffering they cause a child should not be discounted. Meanwhile, the long-term impact of child abuse and neglect on physical health is just beginning to be explored.

The long-term effects can be:

Shaken Baby Syndrome

Shaking a baby is a common form of child abuse that often results in permanent neurological damage (80% of cases) or death (30% of cases). Impaired brain development. Child abuse and neglect have been shown, in some cases, to cause important regions of the brain to fail to form or grow properly, resulting in impaired development. These alterations in brain maturation have long-term consequences for cognitive, language, and academic abilities. NSCAW found more than three-quarters of foster children between 1 and 2 years of age to be at medium to high risk for problems with brain development, as opposed to less than half of children in a control sample.

Poor Physical Health

Several studies have shown a relationship between various forms of household dysfunction (including childhood abuse) and poor health (Flaherty et al., 2006; Felitti, 2002). Adults who experienced abuse or neglect during childhood are more likely to suffer from physical ailments such as allergies, arthritis, asthma, bronchitis, high blood pressure, and ulcers.

Prevention

Government efforts to prevent abuse include home-visitor programs aimed at high-risk families and school-based efforts to teach children how to respond to attempted sexual abuse. Emotional abuse prevention has been promoted through the media.

When children reach age three, parents should begin teaching them about "bad touches" and about confiding in a suitable adult if they are touched or treated in a way that makes them uneasy. Parents also need to exercise caution in hiring babysitters and other caretakers. Anyone who suspects abuse should immediately report those suspicions to the police or his or her local CPS agency, which will usually be listed in the blue pages of the telephone book under Rehabilitative Services or Child and Family Services, or in the yellow pages. Round-the-clock crisis counseling for children and adults is offered by the Childhelp USA/IOF Foresters National Child Abuse Hotline. The National Committee to Prevent Child Abuse is an excellent source of information on the many support groups and other organizations that help abused and at-risk children and their families. One of these organizations, National Parents Anonymous, sponsors 2,100 local self-help groups throughout the United States, Canada, and Europe. Telephone numbers for its local groups are listed in the white pages of the telephone book under Parents Anonymous or can be obtained by calling the national headquarters.

Treatment

Notification of the appropriate authorities, treatment of the child's injuries, and protecting the child from further harm are the immediate priorities in abuse cases. If the child does not require hospital treatment, protection often involves placing him or her with relatives or in foster care. Once the immediate concerns are dealt with, it becomes essential to determine how the child's long-term medical, psychological, educational, and other needs can best be met, a process that involves evaluating not only the child's needs but also the family's (such as for drug abuse counseling or parental skills training). If the child has brothers or sisters, the authorities must determine whether they have been abused as well. On investigation, signs of physical abuse are discovered in about 20% of the brothers and sisters of abused children.

Diagnosis

Doctors and many other professionals who work with children are required by law to report suspected abuse to their state's Child Protective Services (CPS) agency. Abuse investigations often are a group effort involving medical personnel, social workers, police officers, and others. Some hospitals and communities maintain child protection teams that respond to cases of possible abuse. Careful questioning of the parents is crucial, as is interviewing the child. The investigators must ensure, however, that their questioning does not further traumatize the child. A physical examination for signs of abuse or neglect is, of course, always necessary, and may include x -rays, blood tests, and other procedures.

Ethics

One of the most challenging ethical dilemmas arising from child abuse relates to the parental rights of abusive parents or caretakers with regard to their children, particularly in medical settings. In the United States, the 2008 New Hampshire case of Andrew Bedner drew attention to this legal and moral conundrum. Bedner, accused of severely injuring his infant daughter, sued for the right to determine whether or not she remain on life support; keeping her alive, which would have prevented a murder charge, created a motive for Bedner to act that conflicted with the apparent interests of his child. Bioethicists Jacob M. Appel and Thaddeus Mason Pope recently argued, in separate articles, that such cases justify the replacement of the accused parent with an alternative decision-maker.

Child abuse also poses ethical concerns related to confidentiality, as victims may be physically or psychologically unable to report abuse to authorities. Accordingly, many jurisdictions and professional bodies have made exceptions to standard requirements for confidentiality and legal privileges in instances of child abuse. Medical professionals, including doctors, therapists, and other mental health workers typically owe a duty of confidentiality to their patients and clients, either by law and/or the standards of professional ethics, and cannot disclose personal information without the consent of the individual concerned. This duty conflicts with an ethical obligation to protect children from preventable harm.

Accordingly, confidentiality is often waived when these professionals have a good faith suspicion that child abuse or neglect has occurred or is likely to occur and make a report to local child protection authorities. This exception allows professionals to breech confidentiality and make a report even when the child or his/her parent or guardian has specifically instructed to the contrary.

Child abuse is also a common exception to Physician-patient privilege: a medical professional may be called upon to testify in court as to otherwise privileged evidence about suspected child abuse despite the wishes of the child and his/her family.

Many jurisdictions go further with a system of mandated reporters: individuals, typically teachers, medical professionals, mental health workers, athletics coaches, and others, who are required by law to immediately report reasonable suspicion of child abuse or neglect to child welfare authorities. This duty undermines professional autonomy, as a medical professional is required to report even when he/she would prefer not to do so or believes that making a report is not in the best interest of the patient. Reporting is required even in cases where the patient is the suspected abuser, such as if a psychotherapist's patient reports abusing a younger sibling or classmate.

Remedies

- Parents should know the likes and dislikes of their children, should not force them to do which they not like.
- Prevent abuse by both education and by strengthening community.
- Every state should set up a State Commission for the Protection of Rights of the Child and formulate Plans of Action for Child Protection at the district and state levels; should identify vulnerable families and children, prevent vulnerabilities and provide services to those in need.
- A child who has been abused or continues to be in an abusive situation, needs a variety of services, including professional help in the form of trauma counseling, medical treatment, police intervention, and legal supports.
- Awareness on child rights should be spread. Debates and discussion with participation of children can be a regular features on electronic media in order to enhance people's knowledge and sensitivity on child protection issues.
- All children have the right to live in safety and dignity in a protective and nurturing environment, both at home and in the community. This is possible by creating awareness of their rights.
- Discrimination of girls results in their lower enrollment in schools, higher levels of malnutrition, trafficking of girls for sexual exploitation, child

marriage and their non-participation in decision-making in the family etc. These imbalances need to be addressed by bringing about attitudinal changes in people regarding the value of the girl child.

Conclusion

Child abuse has been initiated, the media has started highlighting such issues and an understanding of their gravity is gaining momentum. This understanding must be translated into action, and not only the central government, but state governments, civil society, families and children themselves and they all need to understand the rights perspective and together create the enabling environment wherein a child is protected from abuse and exploitation.

On the contrary, the purpose of the study was to establish that child abuse exists and also to provide the information base that will help government to formulate legislation, schemes and interventions to deal with the problem. The study also throws up key areas for further research.

The primary responsibility of protecting children from abuse and neglect lies with the families or the primary caregivers. However, communities and civil society and all other stakeholders are also responsible for the care and protection of children. The overarching responsibility is that of the state and it is the state that has to create a protective environment and provide a safety net for children who fall into vulnerable and exploitative situations.

References

Amod kanth (1993), " Neglected child", Prayas' Juvenile Aid Centre.

Alex Molnar (1989), "Changing Problem Behaviour in Schools", Jossey Bass Publishers.

Allbright M. (2009), "Mental Health of Children with Hearing Impairments", J. Except Children.

Ellen R. Browning (2000), "Teaching Students with Severe Emotional and Learning Impairments", Allyn and Bacon.

Andrist, L. C. (2003), "American Journal of Maternal Child Nursing".

Mahajan, W. and Madhurima (2001), "Family Violence and Abuse in India", Deep & Deep Publications, New Delhi.

Barnes, H.L & Olson, D.H. (2000), "Child Development".

William C. Morse (1970), "Psychology and Teaching", D.B. Traraporevala Sons & Co.

Sharp, gene (1990), "The Role of Power in Non Violent Struggle", Cambridge, M.A.Albert Einstein Institution.

Mrinalini Somanth (1995), "Psycho-Analytic Approach to Education", Nirmal Publications, *www.pcaiowa.org*

www.vikepedia.com

www.helpguide.org

www.kidsdata.org

www.trible-institute.org

WOMEN ENTREPRENEURS IN UTTAR PRADESH (SPECIAL REFERENCE TO KANPUR AND ALLAHABAD)

*Dinesh Kumar**

This research paper was carried out as the role of women entrepreneurs has gained significance in today's environment. It is based on the women entrepreneurs in and around Kanpur and Allahabad. Women, who succeed as entrepreneurs are risk taking personalities. The women entrepreneurs have their own identity in the world of entrepreneurship. Most of them are capable of fully identifying themselves in their new economic role in society. The sample was selected from two towns, Allahabad and Kanpur. The sample selection was as under: Kanpur - 60% and Allahabad - 40%. This break up was due to the fact that there was a great concentration of available successful women entrepreneur in Kanpur when compared to Allahabad. The paper has highlighted many factors that have motivated women entrepreneurs in starting an entrepreneurial career. Success has been seen mostly among the mid thirty and early forty age group. The government schemes, incentives and subsidies have stimulated and provided support measures to women entrepreneurs in and around the city. In this paper, one of the findings was that while a majority of women came from a family business as a core background and they were mostly married to business families. The business environment seems to have prepared them mentally, thereby facilitating their entry into business. Help and guidance was also available within the family in case of any business problems. Entrepreneurs play very important role in socio-economic welfare of the country. They identify the needs of the business, purchase the other factors of production and coordinate them for some productive purposes. They are the innovators, researchers and risk-takers of the company. Due to the mixed economy in India, both public and private entrepreneurship exists here. Large

* *A/289, Govindpur Colony, Allahabad.*

scale sectors are under the public entrepreneurship. The middle and small scale sectors are under the private entrepreneurship. In order to develop entrepreneurship in this sector, Government of India has stepped towards the Entrepreneurship Development Programmes.

An entrepreneur can be defined as one who initiates and establishes an economic activity or enterprise. Entrepreneurship thus refers to the general trend of setting up new enterprises in a society (Begum, 1993). The International Labor Organization (ILO, 1984, cited in Islam and Aktaruzzaman, 2001) defines an entrepreneur as a person with a set of characteristics that typically includes self-confidence, result-oriented, risk taking, leadership, originality and future-oriented. Khanka (2002) referred to women entrepreneurs as those who innovate, imitate or adopt a business activity. Given that entrepreneurship is the set of activities performed by an entrepreneur, it could be argued that being an entrepreneur precedes entrepreneurship. In any case, the entrepreneurial definitions described above highlight the aspects of risk-taking, innovating and resource organizing.

The paper suggests a new role for women in our economic development. It also provides great potential of accelerating entrepreneurship movement by developing women entrepreneurship. The development of women has become an important issue in present day context. Analyses have so far considered anthropological, social and economic factors, which either inhibit or facilitate women development. A significant trend over the recent years has been towards examining cultural and psychological dimensions of women's role.

This paper also attempted to find the motivational factors that drove these women to become entrepreneurs. It revealed that women do not enter business or industry primarily out of economic factors, or in other words, to make money. The survey indicates that the first and foremost factor listed out by them was "to keep busy," followed by "wanting to fulfill one's ambition", and "pursue one's own interests."

The detailed aspects of these factors along with others will be discussed in the following:

- To identify women who make successful entrepreneurs, their motivational factors and their drive.
- To paper the types of problems they encounter in order to reach the level of success.
- To discover the operational problems they are presently facing.
- To make suitable suggestions for further improvement.

Paper on entrepreneurship has evolved various characteristics that have identified entrepreneurs. A majority (48%) of the respondents were between the ages of 30-42 Years. 45% were married, 10% were divorced, 17% were widows and 28% were single. 60% of the respondents were graduates followed by 5% were undergraduates/diploma holders. 10% of them were postgraduates and 25% were professionally qualified. The majority (55%) belonged to nuclear families and 45% families ware joint but these are matricentric. The figures clearly indicates that despite the common belief that joint families would be more supportive to women who want to branch off on their own and enter in the business, we find that it is the nuclear family which has produced more entrepreneurs. This may be due to the fact that in nuclear setup, the woman has an equal say and is more open to new ideas; also it is easier to convince only one person in the family. 45% of the children of the respondents are in the age group of 11-20 years. As children at this stage do not need the consistent attention, it is quite understandable that women would take to doing something worthwhile to keep themselves busy. An analysis of the occupation backgrounds of the families-pai nts, in-laws and husbands occupations were collected. It is interesting to note that while majority 44% of respondents originally come from service background they are mostly married into business families 45% and where the husbands occupation is also business (41%). Having lived in business environment after marriage, it seems it is easier for these women to take to business rather than any other vocation. This is despite the fact that majority of then belonged to the safer service environment before marriage.

The reasons for which women enter business seem quite different from that of men to become entrepreneurs. In order to arrive at an objective assessment, the respondents ranked 15 possible motivating factors in the order of priority. The weighted scores were accordingly prioritized.

This paper indicates that the need to excel and achieve and the ability to take calculated risk are the prime factors that motivate people. However, this paper indicates different things from the accepted pattern of thinking. Keeping busy has emerged as the dominant factor motivating women entrepreneurs. The data reveals that while 60.8% of respondents have been taking male help in running their enterprises, 39.2% are operating entirely on their own. However, when asked whether they could successfully run their enterprises on their own, 75% said yes.

This is further supported by the fact that majority of respondents were not under economic stress at the time of entering business. "To earn money" has been given the fifth priority. The fact that low priority has been given to "to giving good education to children", "securing social prestige", "making quick money" etc., further substantiates that most of the respondents belong to fairly well to do families. The second and third priorities have been identified as "to fulfill ones' ambition" and "to pursue own interest", which indicates their sense of independence. However, the difference in score between these two factors and the first factor identified is rather significant. Some respondents on their own have indicated "facing challenges" as a motivating factors, but the priority to this factor works out to 6th position with a score of only 16.

The fourth priority was "by accident or circumstances beyond control". This is because of the death of their fathers/husbands. As pointed out earlier a larger percentage of women entrepreneurs have either married into business families or have businessmen as husbands. This could be one of the reasons why, despite having educational qualifications, none of them thought of taking up a job. No priority has been allotted to the factor "no educational qualification for job". 65.2% of women, have approached banks for some kind of financial assistance, 24.1% have depended entirely upon their own capital. The facility taken from banks was basically for working capital limits.

In continuation of the earlier analysis, we find that majority of women (31.3%) have entered business of their own initiative. Although the women had entered business primarily to keep them busy, the idea was generated from their own desire (33.3%). Other factors like advice from family, business family background and availability of finance (26.7%) coupled with their own desire did contribute significantly towards this decision.

It is evident from data that majority of women (48.3%) has gone in for sole proprietorship concerns, followed by partnership concerns (36.7%) and private limited companies (15.03%).

Table 1
Factors Responsible for Choice of Product Line

Factors	*% of total*
High Demand	51.0
Possessing Skills	30.2
Ready market	30.1
Future Prospects	24.0
Requiring creativity	23.9
Typically 'feminine'	17.7
Socially accepted	17.6
Past experience in line	15.5
Family business	13.5
Less Mobility required	11.5
Lower Cost	9.3
Short Gestation period	5.2
High rate of return	5.2
Any other	—

A glance at the first four factors indicates a clear professional attitude towards selection of the product line. This is reinforced by the fact that low priorities have been given to factors like short gestation, high rate of return, lower cost, less mobility required etc. At the same time low priority has also been given to factors like "typically feminine" and "socially accepted" activities. From the sample, it is evident that past experience in the line has been given a low priority (15.5%).

It is generally believed that whenever women venture into business, the preference is given to non-technical or feminine activities involving skills that women generally possess. Along with this, the trend of thinking is that women prefer the safer trading and service industry. However, the Table 2 below dispels these myths.

Table 2
Type of Products Taken by the Respondents

Type of products	*% of total*
Food Products	3.3
Chemical, Rubber & Plastics	8.3
Printing & Paper Products	6.7
Leather	3.3
Handloom & Garments	21.7
Textile	8.3
Beauty Clinics	8.3
Consultancy	5.0
Electronics & Electrical Equipment	13.3
Stainless Steel Utensils	3.3
Machinery	10.0
Other item (Photostat, Wooden toys)	8.3

The survey also proves beyond doubt that women do not stick to the safer trading and service industry. Majority of the sample (70.0%) went in for manufacturing, followed by service industry (16.7%) and trading (13.3%). A further analysis vis-à-vis their educational background reveals that majority of the women who went in for manufacturing was simple graduates (45.2%) followed by undergraduates (31.0%). Very few women (14.3%) had professional qualifications and yet went in for manufacturing. Graduates again had the lead in trading activities. In our sample, 100% of the women who were engaged in trading were graduates. Graduates again accounted for 40.0% of those women engaged in service industry like beauty clinics etc. As a matter of fact, a majority of the sample (51.7%) were graduates, followed by undergraduates (26.7%). Professionals only accounted for 13.3% of the total sample, whereas only 8.3% of women were post-graduates.

The fact that a majority of women are only graduates, and have mostly taken to manufacturing raises a serious doubt about their intentions. Does it mean that the business is only taken lightly, considering most women do not have financial problems? This, coupled with the finding, the majority have entered into business just to keep busy strengthens this premise. This is further strengthened by the fact that 48.3% of the sample had gone in for training, whereas 51.7% were untrained. If their businesses are doing well despite a lack of expertise on their part and an obvious dependency upon others, could they not expect greater gains by professionalism? One sees a sense of complacency in this kind of an attitude.

Table 3
Distribution of Respondents According to Background

Training	*% of total*
Trained Women	48.3
Untrained Women	51.7
Help Taken	% of total
Women operating independently	36.7
Women taking male help	63.3

From the above it is clear that majority of women have to depend upon someone to help them in their day-to-day activities. On enquiries it was found that 36.7% of women have taken no help and are independently running their business, whereas 63.3% of women entrepreneurs do depend upon male help. A look at the table shows a direct correlation between training and dependency upon male help. While this does not mean that it is only trained women who are independent of male help, or vice versa, but clear trend emerges which indicates that with a higher incidence of training, there could be a possibility of with lower dependence on male help.

Training makes entrepreneurs more aware of their environment and of the facilities and incentives offered by the Government, to give encouragement to women entrepreneurs. This evident from the table below:

Table 4
Respondents Awareness to Incentives

	Awareness of Special Incentives			
Training	*Aware*	*Partially Aware*	*Not Aware*	*Total*
Trained	27.6	24.1	48.3	48.3
Untrained	19.4	6.5	74.2	51.7
Total	23.3	15.0	61.7	100.0

Of the trained entrepreneurs 51.7% were either aware or partially aware of the special incentives for women entrepreneurs; where are 74.2% an overwhelming majority of untrained women entrepreneurs, were not at all aware of the incentives meant for them. But it is surprising to note that very few has availed special incentive. On discussions with the respondents, the general feeling was that those incentives only existed in paper and that the formalities for availing then were too many and complicated. On probing deeper, some respondents admitted that they had no time to find out about these schemes. Others who were better read and had subscribed to various journals pertaining to industry finance, management, etc. claimed that no mention of these special incentives appeared anywhere in them. They generally felt that not enough publicity was being given to such incentives to attract women entrepreneurs.

The approach of an entrepreneur, who starts a new enterprise, would be varied, depending on the social and cultural settings. The personality, qualities, the values that sets the goal towards the success, would vary. Every entrepreneur faces some problem in running business and women in our paper are no exception. In the sample almost 15.7% of women said that they did not have any problems.

The majority of the women (84.3%) indicated problems of varied nature. Some of the respondents said that problems arise when dealing with workers. It seems semi-educated or uneducated class of workers cannot visualize a "female boss" in their field of work. The other factors, which have been indicated by the respondents, were marketing, recovery of payments from customers and mobility. The above three factors are related to outside or field jobs which women generally find cumbersome. The problems towards mobility could be multifarious; it could be because of transport, time, distance or other priorities, or even social factors such as insecurity in traveling alone or during late hours, which generally hamper women. Interestingly "honesty" had been indicated as one of the problems. "If you are honest you just cannot do business", this is the way in which most of us do business in India today.

Women are developing confidence to undertake any work, thereby shedding inhibitions. This would encourage many future women entrepreneurs to plunge into business. About 8% of the women felt that problems are less by being women. It was quite heartening to find the majority (56%) of women are aware of their competence.

The remaining 52% of the women felt that woman have to fight harder in the entrepreneurial world. "Business world is cruel and women do not fit in here"; an exporter quoted. Mostly all of them felt that the general competence of women was still suspect. As such they were vulnerable and often exploited. The other kinds of problems were very common as "not being able to work in night shifts, less mobility, less output due to role conflict, etc.".

Every one is subjected to stress because of influence of both organizational and personal situations. Women are subject to a greater stress as the demands of home and career at times causes conflict. As women, they have to strive hard to fulfill their multiple roles. At the same time, they have to project a different image as chief executives of their business. It was found that majority of the respondents (65%) did not suffer from any role conflict. Almost all those who suffered from conflict had children aged between 10 year and 15 years and felt that they were being neglected. They felt that they were not able to fulfill their roles as mother.

Everyone copes with conflict by using some defense or the other. The respondents adopted various strategies in resolving their conflicts stress. It can be seen from the table that women mostly resolved their conflicts by working on priorities (40.0%), the priorities can range from children, husband, home or factory. Most women started work early and finished their work in time for children' return from school, etc.

The next factor "Accepting the situation", 21.7%, which in fact is a positive mechanism. 20.0% cope with the stress by "working harder, this does not indicate a very healthy mechanism to cope with stress. People have generally practiced it and they felt trapped in the activities, which they felt they just had to fulfill. The last 18.3% depend on their faith in God and religion.

Women entrepreneurs enter business predominantly to keep them busy. Although their initial motivation is low, they tend to become high achievers once they get really involved. It was found that while a majority of women came from a family business as a core background and they were mostly married to business families. The business environment seems to have prepared them mentally, thereby facilitating their entry into business. Help and guidance was also available within the family in case of any business problems. Regarding seeking male help, while initially it was taken, at present a majority feels that they can manage entirely on their own. Contrary to general belief, the choice of products by women has not been necessarily "feminine". At the same time, a majority has entered into the complicated and difficult field of manufacturing and related business. Thus women are not security oriented they are ready to take on challenging tasks. The operational problems faced by the women are in the areas of dealing directly with worker and also pertain to difficulties in doing field work. The popular belief has it that women entrepreneurs suffer from role conflict and this exerts a lot of mental tension on her. The survey clearly indicates that this is not true. 65% of women reported as having no conflict. Whatever conflict ever rose was resolved positively by working on priorities and accepting the situation. It was disconcerting to note that despite special incentives available to women entrepreneurs, not even one respondent had availed of it. It was found that some women spent from their own sources without taking any financial help from Government agencies. Majority of women entered business without any relevant training. It is heartening to note that women do not face problems by virtue of they being women. Some of them feel that it is advantageous for them. It is been proved beyond doubt that women entrepreneurs do enjoy respect in the society.

There is need for training the already existing women entrepreneurs, in the various aspects of management. The Government must make greater efforts to publicize the various schemes announced from time to time to attract women entrepreneurs.

References

Anderson, Ellen (June 1984), "Why aren't there more Women Managers?" World Executive Digest.

Weber, M. (2001), (Revised edition 2001), The Protestant Ethic and the Spirit of Capitalism. London: Routledge.

DOMESTIC VIOLENCE EXPERIENCED BY WORKING AND NON-WORKING WOMEN IN URBAN AND RURAL AREAS OF JAMMU REGION

Bharti Prabhakar[*] *& Nidhi Kotwal*[**]

Introduction

The problem of violence against women is not new. Women in the Indian society have been victims of humiliation, torture and exploitation. In spite of the legislative measures adopted in favor of women in our society after independence, the spread of education and women's gradual economic independence, countless women still continue to be the victims of violence. They are beaten, kidnapped, raped, burnt and murdered. Violence against women may be categorized as:

(i) Criminal violence- rape, abduction, murder....

(ii) Domestic violence- dowry deaths, wife battering, sexual abuse, maltreatment....

(iii) Social violence- forcing the wife/daughter-in-law to go for female foeticide, eve-teasing, refusing to give a share to women in property......

The term domestic violence is wide and encompasses in its scope the types of violence resorted to within the home. The overwhelming majority of victims of domestic violence are women. Domestic violence not only includes conduct which amount to cruelty on a woman by her husband or any of his relative but also includes any act which is unbecoming of the brutally beaten or abused by their husbands or in-laws. Domestic violence is a slow poison which is swallowing the ingredients of family life. Domestic violence is a serious human

* *Project Officer, Department of Lifelong Learning, University of Jammu, Jammu*

** *P.G. Department of Home Science (CRM and E), GCW Parade, Jammu, Jammu and Kashmir, India*

threat to women in every society- rich and poor, developed and industrialized particularly in patriarchal societies. It is used as a weapon for subjugating women and suppressing their rights as equal partners in the family structure. Domestic violence is widespread and cuts across caste, creed, class and all educational levels. Domestic violence strikes in various forms- physical, sexual, emotional and psychological.

In United States, a woman is beaten every 18 minutes. In Peru 70% of all crimes reported to the Police involve women beaten by their husbands. According to human rights commission of Pakistan in the 400 cases of domestic violence reported in 1993 in the province of Punjab. Nearly half ended with the death of a wife.

However a more recent International Centre for Research on women (ICRW) study, 2002, conducted on men, masculinity and domestic violence in 4 Indian states finds that men are not naturally violent.

Men have always been taught to perceive themselves as the superior sex, says Jyotsana Chatterjee, Director, Joint Women's Programme, Delhi. It is the conditioning she says that makes them believe that they have control over their wives. Violence affects the lives of millions of women worldwide. Violence against women is a universal problem and it continues to grow. With these in mind the study was taken up with the objective- (i) to study the domestic violence experienced by working and non working women in rural and urban areas, (ii) whom they approached in seeking help.

Methodology

Sample for rural areas was drawn from 4 villages (Ratanpur, Pounichak, Ramgarh and Ambgrota) and sample for urban was drawn from different areas of Jammu city. 250 working and 250 non-working women were selected purposively from each area; hence a total of 1000 women formed the sample of the study. The data was collected in the month of April- May, 2007. An interview schedule was used for data collection. To analyze the data, collected information was classified in the light of objectives set forth for the study.

Results and Discussion

Respondents Experience of Domestic Violence

Table 1 shows that majority of the respondents in both the settings irrespective of their working status reported that they were mostly harassed by their mother-in-laws. They were denied food; good place to sleep and were verbally abused for every small thing. Violence towards women in the context of marriage becomes more significant when a husband who is supposed to love and protect his wife beats her. For a woman, being battered by a man whom she trusted most becomes a shattering experience. The violence can range from slaps and kicks to broken bones, torture and attempted murder and even murder itself. Sometimes the violence may be related to drunkenness but not always. 52% of urban non-working and 36% urban working and 34% rural non-working and 28% rural working women stated that they were physically and verbally abused by their husbands in the presence of others for not following his instructions. The women cried and prayed when their husbands were violent. They were worried about their children when their husbands became abusive. The Women reported that they stayed in the marriage for the sake of their children. Some of the women stated that their husbands forced them when they were drunk. Statistics reveal that 45% of Indian women are slapped, kicked or beaten by their husbands (A study conducted by International Centre for Research on women ICRW 2000).

Father-in-law, Sister-in-law, Brother-in-law were also reported to verbally and physically abuse the women.

Table 1
Respondents Experience of Domestic Violence

	Urban				*Rural*			
	Working women		*Non-working women*		*Working women*		*Non-working women*	
	N	*%*	*N*	*%*	*N*	*%*	*N*	*%*
At the hands of Father-in-law	70	28%	140	56%	80	32%	80	32%
At the hands of Mother-in-law	150	60%	157	62.8%	140	56%	190	76%
At the hands of Sister-in-law	50	20%	40	16%	17	6.8%	120	48%
At the hands of Brother-in-law	30	12%	20	8%	30	12%	40	16%
At the hands of Husband	90	36%	130	52%	70	28%	85	34%
Other Relatives	40	16%	50	20%	100	40%	137	54.8%

Helped Seeked From

In Indian culture, a wife rarely thinks in terms of reporting a case of battering to the police. She suffers humiliation in silence and takes it as her destiny. Even if she wants to revolt, she cannot do it because of the fear that her own parents would refuse to keep her in their house permanently after the marital break down. Table 2 depicts that majority of the women from urban areas stated that they discussed their domestic issues with the relatives and took help from them. Where as women in rural areas solved their problems on their own. These Women stated that they could not afford to make it public as this would affect the status of the family, moreover, they did not want their children to suffer. None of the sample seeked the help of any agency like- police, NGO's or women cells. Goel (2004) stated that 90% of domestic violence goes unreported.

Table 2
Help Seek From

	Urban				*Rural*			
	Working women		*Non-working women*		*Working women*		*Non-working women*	
	N	*%*	*N*	*%*	*N*	*%*	*N*	*%*
Police	-	-	-	-	-	-	-	-
NGO's	-	-	-	-	-	-	-	-
Women Cells	20	.08%	-	-	-	-	-	-
Relatives	100	40%	150	60%	50	20%	50	20%
Neighbors	80	32%			20	.08%		
No One	50	20%	100	40%	180	72%	200	80%

Conclusion

Women have suffered discrimination and been the victims of atrocities for long. A conscious and compassionate vision is needed to evaluate and assess the mental condition of women subjected violence. Wife abuse is not a recent phenomenon. Its roots can be traced to the remote past. It was found that women suffered varying degrees of physical as well as psychological violence by their husbands. A victim of domestic violence would experience even routine tasks such as daily chores and child care as insurmountable mainly because of fatigue, chronic headaches, infections or depression. Men should overcome patriarchal beliefs and get involved in the process of establishing gender equity. The process of sensitizing men on the issue of domestic violence should start from early childhood itself. There should be at least one shelter home in every city. Indigenous arbitration bodies like mahila mandals and self help groups. should be formed in each locality to combat the problem of domestic violence locally. So, it could be concluded that domestic violence makes the life worse for all especially for women.

Suggesstions

Change is needed in the perception of the society towards dignity of women she should be treated at par with her male counterpart because threat to male authority is the main cause of domestic violence against women.

Violence against women is primarily a gender issue so awareness against gender biases is necessary to minimize the problem. Legal education to fight against justice must be imparted to girls at high school or secondary school level so that they stand up and fight for their rights.

Women in general should be educated about their rights and also about the agency to be approached if they have any problem of violence in their family.

Family counseling centre must be set up at lower levels so that families at risk may be identified and thorough counseling support and help may be given to such families before it takes the shape of conflict.

References

Goel, A. (2004), "Violence and Protecting Measures for Women Development and Empowerment", New Delhi. Deep and Deep Publications Private Limited, 124-153

Kotwal, N. (2007), "Awareness of Women's Right Among Working and Non-working Women of Urban and Rural Areas of Jammu Region", (Project Report Submitted to the UGC) National Council for Women: Annual Report 2000-2001, New Delhi, 32-33.

Singh, D. (2002), "Mitigating Violence Against Women in Social Welfare", 511-519.

Siddiqi, F.E. and Ranganathan, S. (2001), "Women and Human Rights" (A Guide for Social Activities), part 2. New Delhi. Kanishka Publishers.

DCWC Research Bulletin Vol. 1X Issue 3 July-September 2005, *Documentation Centre on Women and Children (DCWC)*National Institute of Public cooperation and Child Development (NIPCCD) 5, Siri Institutional Area, Hauz Khas New Delhi-110016.

VIOLENCE AGAINST KENYAN WOMEN'S – SOME ISSUES

S. B. Akash & Bichanga Evans***

Introduction

Women experience discrimination and oppression in every culture. There is no society where they are treated as equals to men. Some of the offences like domestic violence or rape are global problems. Others are found in specific cultural contexts. In this paper, we describe problems that are related to customs practiced in Kenya. The role of traditional models, access to education, leadership positions, in heritance of land, beating as a sign of appreciation, polygamy, barrenness, wife inheritance, child marriages', female circumcision, Food taboos. Not everybody links these issues are women discrimination. Others say some customs have become oppressive in the modern context. Women are becoming more conscious about discriminating behaviour and structures that oppress them and are articulating more openly their expectations to be treated as equals. They feel supported by international awareness that has found concrete in the universal declaration of human rights. In 1981 Organization of African Unity (OAU) published the African charter on human and people's rights, a charter that took into consideration the specific African context. Concerning the protection of women, as stipulated in article 18.3 which states that, the state shall eliminate discrimination against women and also ensures the protection of the rights of the woman and the child.

A woman's right to own, inherit, manage and dispose property in Kenya is greatly impeded by discriminatory customary laws, biased attitudes, prevailing social stigmas, and

* *Associate Professor, Dept., of Commerce, Kuvempu University, Shankaraghatta.*

** *Scholar Dept. of Commerce, Kuvempu University, Shankaraghatta*

a lack of awareness, resources and access to formal legal services among women. Although land and inheritance rights for widows are acknowledged in statute, they remain unequal to those of men who lose their spouses, and realizing these rights can be challenging in a country that also recognizes colonial, customary and religious laws. Women's property rights violations become even more widespread in the context of HIV/AIDS-related death, when a woman can be blamed for her husband's death, and her access to justice further obstructed by complex and expensive legal structures, attitudes within legal services institutions, and the under-representation of women in governance structures. Outdated property titling systems often grant title to men rather than women, or can be too costly for poor women to access.

Objectives of the Study

1. To study the awareness level of women's against violations of their rights.
2. To study the role of NGOs in creating awareness amongst the women's to minimize their violations.
3. To analyze the education role in order to over come the problems faced by women's.

Methodology

This section basically presents the general procedure for carrying out the study. A description of the design and appropriate methodology adopted in carrying out the study is done. Characteristics of the study population as well as sampling design and procedures are discussed include sources of data and administration of data collected.

The study relied on both primary data and secondary data in establishing the needed relationship between the different variables involved on the study of violations against women rights in Kenya. The research was a personal experience with women from different parts of country and age groups, men too were interviewed on some family issues. Some questions were asked to young women via face book on how they would respond to women violations.

Sources of Data

The study is based on both primary and secondary data. The primary data collected from the sample Kenyan women's with the help of structured interview scheduled in order to gather required information to attain research objectives.. The secondary data was ascertained from related literatures in the study area. The sources were journals, books, websites, NGOS reports and government reports.

Somte Issues that Lead to Violations of Women Rights in Kenya

A complex blend of discriminatory laws and customs combined with insensitive institutions, widespread ignorance of their rights and other obstacles have guaranteed that in comparison to her male counterpart, the average Kenyan woman is disadvantaged at every stage in life, seen right from birth. While the birth of a male child is greeted with much admiration, dance and feasting, there are no similar celebrations to mark the birth of a female child. Most of Kenyan families would rather invest in a boy's education or development because in due course, a girl will get married and 'go away'. Unfortunately for her, by the time she 'goes away'; her marital clan will be looking to her for children, additional labour and generally as a resource around the homestead. Her personal development will not be their priority.

In the upbringing of children, boys are generally given preferential treatment as compared to their female siblings, to the extent of sometimes marrying off a girl for the sole purpose of using some of the bride price (cattle and in recent times money paid to a woman's family in exchange for her hand in marriage) to educate and provide for her brother(s) needs.

The preference of education is given to a male child was the question many women gave their opinions and represented in the table below:

Table 1
Opinion of the Respondents Towards Preference given to Educating their Children

Preference	*No. of women respondents*	*Percentage*
Male child	156	76
Female child	54	24
Total	210	100

Source: Field study.

76 per cent of the respondents said there is has been a tendency that male child is given preference for education than the female child represented by 24 per cent. This was saddening to most of the women who said even if it's proved that the female child is intelligent than the male child, the society still regards him above her.

Compared to boys, girls face special challenges in their pursuit of academic excellence. For instance, unlike boys who are exempted from domestic chores, girls must do their share of housework while away from school. They, therefore, have very little recreation or free time to invest in academic pursuits. Boys, on the other hand, have plenty of time to rest and further their academic interests and are generally better informed than their female counterparts. Unfortunately, this is interpreted to mean that boys are academically superior in comparison to girls. Consequently, girls receive less education than boys at every level and women's literacy rate (76%) is lower than men's (89%). When they finally get to the job market, women find themselves at a disadvantage compared to their male counterparts - they are generally less educated and have scored less than their male counterparts. In addition to their economically viable jobs, they will have to perform basic domestic duties and are usually fatigued in the office unlike their male counterparts. This is wrongly interpreted to mean that men are more productive. These reasons, coupled with insensitive institutions and deeply entrenched discrimination against women explain why most of them are engaged in low prestige jobs, earning an average salary of less than half that of similarly qualified male colleagues.

Culture

Kenya has a diverse ethnic heritage with more than forty-two ethnic communities. Each of these has cultural practices that tend to infringe on the women's human rights. Female Genital Mutilation is still practiced in some communities, for example, Kisii, Pokot, Maasai, Marakwet, and Somali amongst others. For some of these communities, immediately after the cut they are forced to get married to old men they do not even know without the mothers' consent. There have been cases of girls as young as eight years old being married off to very old men. In others, the girl will not get a husband if she is not circumcised. The cut not only affects their childbirth but they also get infections as a result of the leaking waste.

Inconclusive studies have shown that female Genital Mutilation season contributes to the rise in armed conflicts as the men have to bring livestock as dowry, therefore, they engage in raids to acquire the same when they do not have them. Bride price or dowry is a part of culture that was traditionally meant to be an exchange of gifts in appreciation and also served to unify both families. It has since become commercialized and this has been to the detriment of women's human rights. Men view their wives to be their property. Due some pressures from government and non -governmental bodies this culture has seen some declining trend.

Polygamy

Polygamy is viewed as an acceptable culture in most communities in Kenya either formally or informally. This encourages a culture of extra-marital affairs, which then exposes women to HIV/AIDS and STDs. A complaint from a wife who is dissatisfied may result in physical abuse. If the woman is beaten, she has nowhere to turn as it is viewed to be a domestic case and, therefore, not viewed with seriousness. In some cases it is referred to customary law, which discriminates against women's human rights.

In other communities, women are not expected to eat well and they are brought up believing that they are worth nothing and that the man is a superior human. To this date, these women are seen to perpetuate the same inferiority culture by teaching their daughters the same things they learnt. Certain cultural groups in Kenya violate women's human rights by chasing the woman away when she has twins.

Wife Inheritance

Wife inheritance, which is the succeeding/taking over of a woman after the death of the husband, it is still prevalent in some communities in the Western and Nyanza Provinces of Kenya. Women are not given a choice. As a result of this, the woman has to go through several rights. For example, the woman has to be cleansed through a 'professional' cleanser, who is supposed to be insane. The woman is, therefore, exposed to HIV and STIs or may transmit them herself if she is a carrier. This negatively impacts on health and life expectancy.

In some communities, if the husband dies before they have moved into a new house then she is forced to sleep on top of the corpse as a ritual. In the same way, if the wife dies before they have moved into the new house then the husband also has to sleep on top of his wife's corpse. This is one of the few negative cultural practices where the man and woman are given equal treatment.

Generally speaking, language is used to portray women negatively. Anything nasty and diminishing is compared to the woman. For example, one may overhear men saying, 'you are behaving like a woman' when they are being foolish or cowardly. Or any child who is not performing well in school or is misbehaving is claimed to have taken after the mother.

Customary Law

Customary laws, which are formally recognized under Kenyan law impact more profoundly on the lives of women than statutory law. These are mostly unwritten and constantly evolving norms that derive legitimacy from tradition and custom rather than an Act of Parliament. Customary laws are fluid and prone to subjective interpretation. Inevitably, those interpreting customary law bring has some biases and women unfriendly.

Domestic Violence

Domestic violence is defined as abuse involving intimate partners, which occurs in a domestic setting, especially the home. It is the most common cause of injury to women in Kenya. It usually includes physical violence, emotional, sexual and verbal abuse, and neglect. Domestic violence is widespread in Kenyan society under various circumstances in the household, husband to the wife; husband to the children, mother-in-law to daughter-in-law; incest and defiling of children. Most of the latter cases go unreported because of culture. It is culturally acceptable to simply kill or slaughter animals to cleanse the father and child, and once it is done it is felt to be okay. The mothers also perpetuate these violations as they do not speak about it and healing does not effectively take place. The victims are often threatened to keep quiet to avoid shaming the family.

Table 2
Opinions of Women's Towards Different Violations

Categories	*No. of women affected*	*Percentage*
Verbal/psychological	90	43
Physical violence	70	33
Sexual violence	50	24
Total	210	100

Sources: Field survey.

By studying the categories of physical violence, sexual violence and verbal/psychological violence, it can be observed from the above table that verbal/psychological violence affects 43% of the women; physical violence affects 33% and sexual violence against women accounts for 24%.

Table 3
Level of Education and Opinions Towards Violation

Level of Education	*No. of women affected*	*Percentage*
PUC	30	14
Diploma	40	19
Graduation	50	24
Post Graduation	90	43
Total	210	100

Sources: Field survey.

Among the women who reported having experienced physical violence from their husband/companion, the highest percentage (43%) involved those who had post graduation degree, women who are educated are difficult to handle, hence sharing of responsibilities even those which are performed by them to men. The graduation group with 24 per cent also experienced the same. It is clear that as the level of education increases the abuse also increases. As far as the presence of children during violent incidents is concerned, 49.2 per cent of the respondents who admit to being the victims of violence indicate that their children never witness such scenes, while 28.4 per cent admit that violence occurs sometimes or often in their presence.

As a result of domestic violence women end up severely psychologically affected. They have feelings of shame and guilt and suffer depression and anxiety disorders. Many feel trapped, not knowing what to do. There have been cases of women killing themselves and other cases of where women kill their children first then commit suicide. Children are also psychologically affected with the results of poor academic performance, drug addiction, negative behavioural changes and more often than naught male children of domestic abusers tend to perpetuate it when they are married.

Sexual Violence

Sexual violence against women and children has been alarmingly on the increase. This includes indecent assault; rape; sexual harassment; and intercourse that have become a requirement before women can be employed. Sexual violence against women has especially been on the increase in the public domain and even the private domain. Many at times all this violations are unreported for one reason or the other.

Table 4
Sexual Violations Persons Convicted for Sex Offences

	1980	*1990*	*1995*	*2000*
Women	42 (9.3)	55 (8.7)	53 (8.4)	61 (7.2)
Men	411 (92.7)	577 (91.3)	575 (91.6)	791 (92.7)
Total	453	632	628	852

Sources: Government Report.

Kenya has made remarkable progress in social indicators over the past decade. Hence, this has shown some remarkable decrease on the number of people convicted against sex offences. In 1980 there were 42 cases reported representing 9.3 per cent, 8.7, 8.4 and 7.2 per cent respectively in 1990, 1995 and 2000. Enrolment in education has increased from 66.2% in 1994 to 74.2% in 2004; adult literacy increased from 52.3% to 65.7% during the same period; life expectancy at birth has also increased by 6%, and there has been a remarkable decrease in the infant and maternity mortality rate. However, there is indeed a gender gap in many aspects of life.

Sexual Harassment

In Kenya women have claimed to have experienced some sexual harassment at work, but only a few of them have reported such incidents to the official authorities. In most cases the perpetrator of the sexual harassment are colleagues, superiors and police.

Table 5
Opinions of Respondents Towards Incidences Leading to Sexual Harassment

Incidences	*No. of women affected*	*Percentage*
Pressure to start a relationship	30	14
Sexual innuendos/jokes	50	24
Persistent pressure for a date	60	29
Physical contact(touch)	20	10
Sexual intercourse pressures	15	07
Provocative gestures	35	17
Total	210	100

Sources: Field Survey.

From the table above it can be concluded that the most common incidences of sexual harassment involve unwelcome sexual attention, jokes, comments, questions, unwelcome staring, gestures and whistling. 29% of the incidents involve persistent pressure for a date, 23% sexual innuendos/jokes, 17% provocative gestures, 14% pressure to start a relationship, 10% undesirable physical contact - touching and 07% pressure to engage in sexual intercourse. All these incidences can be committed either at the work places (offices) on streets, common meeting places, learning institutions and during some festive periods. And in the most cases the majorities of perpetrators are men. Who are either the bosses in companies, parastatals and learning institutions. There are cases where ladies are awarded marks by professors after being used to satiate the sexual desires of the lecturers.

Although the Kenyan Constitution calls for the equality of men and women, women are discriminated against in many areas of life. They are deprived of their human rights. The existing culture is a major factor in the "persistence of traditional male-dominated society". Another very important factor is the poor social and economic status of women. This status not only affects women's rate of educational attainment and employment, but also their vulnerability to violence.

Table 6
Nature of Domestic Violation

Modes	*No. of women affected*	*Percentage*
Abusive behaviour from husband (Verbal)	118	56
Psychological	92	44
Total	210	100

Source: Field Survey.

From the table above 56% and 44% of women have sometimes or often experience abusive behaviour from their husband/companion in the form of verbal or psychological violence, when this is compared with the places where the women reside 63% of women residing in sub-urban centers sometimes or often experience abusive behaviour from their husband/companion in the form of verbal or psychological violence. The equivalent percentage of women residing in rural areas reaches 37%. The other question which was posed to the respondents and especially those who are married to confirm of the fact of physical and psychological abuse meted to them. 38% of women, belonging to the age group of 25-30 confirmed that they have experienced verbal/ psychological violence. This was expected, since most of these groups are young and have more expectations into marriage. 24% also had the same experience. 19% of the women belonging to the age group of 41-45 also experienced the same but majority said its normal life to them. 14% of the other women experienced verbal and psychological torture, this is the group which is hard to understand marriage life and always there are more comparisons to their

Table 7
Selected Demographical Factors and Violation

Demographical Factors		
Geographical Background		
Urban Centers	132	63
Rural Areas	78	37
Total	210	100
Age group		
18-24	30	14
25-30	80	38
31-36	50	24
37-40	40	19
Above 41	10	5
Total	210	100

parents. The age group of 41 above had little misunderstandings, since they have settled in life.

Causes of Gender-Based Violence

(a) *Exercise of power and control:* The perpetrator has a strong desire to exercise power and control over the victim.

(b) *Society and culture:* Many people think it is 'natural' for a man to have control over a woman in an intimate relationship.

(c) *Parental Influence:* As they are growing up, many batterers observe that violent behaviour gives the violent personal total power within the family.

(d) *False beliefs:* For example, in the African culture a man should beat his wife, that violent men are protectors, that men who beat their wives love them, that women should be disciplined when at fault.

Economic Status

Those who bear the brunt of corruption are the powerless and voiceless poor, majority of who are women. Corruption deprives women of basic services and human rights such as shelter, food, education, health and employment. Currently there are five bodies in place to fight corruption at the behest of the government. They are all independent and spending taxpayers money to pay their staff. As a nation we are spending much-needed money on institutions that have thus far not yielded much in terms of persecution. On the other hand, there was a massive cleanup of the judiciary that saw corrupt judges being suspended pending investigations. Many opted to resign rather than endure the commissions of inquiry.

Women's human rights are often violated in the workplace. For example, the case of the Export Processing Zone where women workers are subjected to long working hours and very low pay; when they get pregnant there are no considerations given to them, they still have to work long hours and there is no maternity leave, therefore, they have to return to work as soon they deliver; they do not get paid on time; they are sexually harassed to keep their jobs. For women working in the farms, there is no protective gear from the harmful chemicals they use to spray on the crops; they are not insured. The government is not giving any interventions for this.

Disinheritance

There is a deep rooted tradition in rural areas that only male heirs may inherit, especially assets like land and buildings. This is due to the perception of women, not as individuals, but rather as dependents on a father, husband or brother. Another related reason is that a married woman who inherited from her family's estate would be perceived as taking assets that rightly belonged to her male relatives and giving them to her husband. In some cases, disinheritance is undertaken legally by making a will or donating assets to the preferred beneficiary before death. However, in other cases, the male family members just refuse to implement the law.

Women's rights to property in Kenya are unequal to that of men. Their rights to own, inherit, manage and dispose of property are under attack from customs, laws and individuals including government officials who believe that women cannot be trusted with property or do not deserve property. The effects of property rights violations harm women, their children and Kenya's overall development. A woman's access to property depends on her relationship to the man.

Table 8
Reasons Responsible for Sexual Harassment

Reasons	*No. of women affected*	*Percentage*
Promotions	70	33
Pass exam	61	29
Better pay	19	09
Retain job	60	29
Total	210	100

Sources: Primary survey.

From the table above, it clear that most of the women who are sexually harassed 33% give in because they want promotions and 29 % in order to retain their status or positions rather than being dismissed. This is the case of those who are working in parastatals or companies in order to be favoured by their bosses. 29 % are those who are in studying institutions colleges, universities and even high schools, who oblige in order to pass their exams or get higher marks. Most of these sexual cases occur when nobody else is present apart from the perpetrator and the victim.

Table 9
Sources that Used by Respondents to Share About their Sexual Harassment

Share experience	*No. Respondents*	%
Friends	60	29
Family	80	38
Colleagues	51	24
Kept silent	19	9
Total	210	100

Sources: Primary survey.

As regard to sharing of the experience of sexual harassment 38% of women who experience sexual harassment in their working environment share this unpleasant experience with family members. Whereas 29% share it with the friends, 24% of share it with their colleagues to make them realize what is going on, and urge them to kept their distance and the other 9% of female-victims of sexual harassment report being aware that the perpetrator had harassed other women in their working environment but kept silent, due fear of victimization.

Right to Education

One of the major hindrances to the girl's right to education is forced marriage. This is defined as the act of forcefully taking a girl, who is below the age of 18 years, from her parents/guardians and making her a wife. This is an offence under the Children's Act. It has serious effects on the girl as it stops her physical and mental development, which is mainly dropping out of school.

Cultural practices of female circumcisions where the girl is married off as soon as the cut is done also negatively impact in girls' access to education. A girl's right to education has become a reality in some parts, due government and some NGO intervention. However, where girls are forced to drop out of school or not go all-together as a result of harmful cultural practices, there has not been much of a positive impact on their right to education. Schools have been set up by local civil society groups near or around communities where girls are being forced into early marriage and some have been successful in rescuing several girls from this plight. However, reports indicate that in one area of the North Rift, girls that had been rescued from female circumcision were forced to return back to their families with intimidation from a Member of Parliament, who is a woman and happens to have been fortunate to run away to avoid the cut when she was a girl. This is a case of how women are their own worst enemies when it comes to the violations of women's human rights.

Challenges

Following are some of the challenges impacting negatively on women's human rights: The delay in the passing of the new constitution jeopardizes the hope of the women, as there are so many recommendations that can create change for the better. There are several bills that are waiting to be debated and passed into law. For example, the Domestic Violence Bill, which is supposed to address violence within the f mily; Affirmative Action Bill, which is supposed to enhance the position of women in Kenya by correcting the gender imbalance in Kenya in Parliament and government positions; Criminal Law Amendment Act, whose objective is to harmonize penalties relating to sexual offences. These bills are taking too long to be discussed and passed into law. The lack of political will to domesticate all the ratified international and regional human rights' instruments on the part of government.

Civil society actors have been given several government appointments and this has left civil society weakened and in need of recreating our image as well as ensuring that it is not individual-centered, which has mostly been the case to date, but organization-centered to ensure continuity. The proliferation of small arms and light weapons that exacerbates armed violence is a challenge to peace and security in the nation, which on the whole results in the violations of women's human rights. There needs to be coordinated efforts by the government to secure the porous borders, as well as the improvement of the terms of employment for the police who have been known to liaise with criminal groups to exchange weapons for money.

Civil Society

There are numerous women's organizations and organizations focusing on women's human rights in Kenya. They are involved in various activities, some of which include: providing legal services for women who are not in a position to afford it, peace building and conflict transformation training, training the police force to be sensitive when handling victims of sexual and domestic violence, lobbying for the provision of a women's desk in each police station, which is yet to be fully implemented, raising the awareness of women on their rights, providing temporary shelters and rescue centre's to victims of harmful cultural practices and abuse, and empowering women amongst others.

The Government's framework to promote women's human rights is the Women's Bureau. It is a government department, which has the role of furthering the commitments made, by the government for the enhancement of women's rights. Serious questions regarding the capacity of the bureau to undertake these functions led to gender activists' agitating for the enactment of a law to establish a National Gender Commission. A bill for the same has been drafted and is currently in Parliament awaiting debate. The draft constitution also provides for the establishment of a constitutional gender commission.

Conclusions

From the foregoing discussion it is clear that women's were exploited in different ways in Kenya , that's why it is not good for wellbeing of women's hence Kenyan government should match existing legislation and pass new laws to account for women's rights. In order to ensure that women do not face destitution in the event of divorce or the death of a spouse. It should ensure equal access and control of property by women, particularly widows, and outlaw harmful, dangerous, and degrading practices such as widow's inheritance and ritual cleansing. The Kenyan government should also take a holistic and respectful approach to its response to the HIV/AIDS crisis; most critically, it must reevaluate or repeal laws which criminalize HIV/AIDS and place women at particular risk for prosecution. Such action is not only an obligation under ICESCR and is within the direct power of the Kenyan government, but would considerably advance the goal of economic, social, and cultural rights for all citizens of Kenya. In conclusion, as the women of Kenya look forward to the day when, 'nations will be judged not by their military or economic strength nor by the splendor of their capital cities, and their public buildings, but the well-being of their peoples, by their ability to participate in the decisions that affect their lives and the protection that is afforded to their women'. It is time for all the Kenyan women, and indeed all African women, to arise and shine for their time has come.

References

Republic of Kenya, National Development Plan 1997-2001 (Nairobi: Government Printer 1997), p. 146.

United Nations Development Program (UNDP), Human Development Report 2002 New York: UNDP, 2002, p. 224

Concluding Comments of the Committee on the Elimination of Discrimination against Women: Kenya, UN Doc. CEDAW/C/KEN/CO/6, Para. 21.

Report of the Commission of Inquiry into Post-Election Violence, October 2008, p. 263.

World Health Organization (WHO) (1979), Khartoum Seminar on Traditional Practices Affecting the Health of Women and Children, Khartoum, Sudan.

Organization of African Unity, African Charter on the Rights and Welfare of the Child, 1990, Article 24(3).

United Nations (UN), Report of the International Conference on Population and Development, New York, 1994.

UN, Report of the Fourth World Conference on Women, New York, 1995.

C. W. Dugger, "A Refugee's Body Is Intact but Her Family Is Torn," *New York Times*, Sept. 11, 1996, pp. A1, B6-B7.

BAN ON BURQA
PIERCING THE VEIL

*Charu Modi**

This paper is without prejudice to any religious, social or cultural sentiment related to Islam, and is a mere analysis of the author.

Introduction

The question with regards to legitimacy of burqa is a burning issue throughout the world, especially after an absolute ban by France. Countries are under a dilemma to second France or not. The ban has been imposed due to many considerations like oppression of women, hindrance in development, discrimination issues, security reasons etc. But the question to be discussed is, as to what extent a blanket ban is valid? And moreover, are these reasons justifiable for the ban on a religious practice? The wearing of the *Hijab* or the *Burqa* is currently an issue in Singapore, Germany, Egypt, Russia, Italy, Holland and Turkey, and many other countries.[1] There are few countries who have levied ban on some specific religious symbols or at some specific occasions only, like at Airports for security check or for getting an ID card etc.

The next moot question here is that, is India in a position to impose such a ban? Would that be successful or it would cause only communal problems...etc? The paper briefly discusses the provisions of the holy Quran related to or alleged to be related to burqa, social consequences of burqa and legal consequences of burqa ban etc.

Burqa in Islam: A Debate

There has been a disagreement in Islamic circles as to what extent does Quran advocate the wearing of Burqa. It is widely

* *Room No. 11, Girls' Hostel, Dr. Ram Manohar Lohiya National Law University, Sector D-1, L.D.A. Colony, Kanpur Road Scheme, Lucknow (U.P.)*

accepted in intellectual circles that the Quran does not specifically mention the Burqa or instructs women to wear such extremely confining clothes. Although the burqa and other Muslim Coverings are attributed to several passages of the Qur'an discussing modesty and sexual temptations[2], many well known Muslim scholars across the globe disagree that the burqa is in fact a religious practice.[3] Instead most agree that it is a cultural practice rather than religious.[4] Some Muslims even refute the notion that the Hadith support the burqa. Gammal Banna, an Egyptian author of several books regarding the rights of Muslim women, challenged the legitimacy of extreme attempts at modesty when he stated that "[n]either the Qur'an nor the Hadith require women to wear a head scarf", that practice simply "derives from a erroneous reading of the Quran."[5] Rather the Holy Quran requires women to be modest in their clothings and makes no refernce to Burqa.

Chapter 24, Verse 31:

"And tell the believing women to lower their gaze and be modest, and to display of their adornment only that which is apparent, and to draw their veils over their bosoms, and not to reveal their adornment save to their own husbands or fathers or husbands' fathers, or their sons or their husbands' sons, or their brothers or their brothers' sons or sisters' sons, or their women, or their slaves, or male attendants who lack vigour, or children who know naught of women's nakedness. And let them not stamp their feet so as to reveal what they hide of their adornment. And turn unto Allah together, O believers, in order that ye may succeed."

On the other hand, scholars claim that Quran provides for such coverings which protect the body of women from the gaze of other men. They also reflect the opinion that Islamic principles and practices can never be seen as blind impositions but they are a rational source of personal morality which the individual is free to follow. Moreover, not following these practices does not attract penalty and as such is not provided by the Holy Qur'an.

Chapter 33, Verse 59:

"O Prophet! Tell thy wives and daughters, and the believing women, that they should cast their outer garments over their persons: that is most convenient, that they should be known (as such) and not molested".

The debate on this somber issue is endless as the interpretations of Qur'an are differently done and it concerns the right of freedom of religion of a major group of world society.

International Obligations

On one hand State has an obligation to protect the freedom of religion and freedom of free speech and expression of persons residing in its territory. Therefore, giving a right to Muslims as a whole to profess and practice their own Islamic religion. On the other hand, the State is also obliged to protect women oppression and discrimination due to these traditional practices and customs. And this gives a valid authority to the State to ban such practices.

The State is under an obligation to protect the religious rights of every individual under following Human Rights Treaties:

> *"Everyone has the right to freedom of thought, conscience and religion..."*[6]

Simultaneously, International Obligation on states to safeguard the victims of discrimination is derived from:

> *"Everyone is entitled to all the rights and freedoms set forth in this Declaration, without distinction of any kind, such as race, colour, sex, language, religion..."*[7]

CEDAW specifically addressed to issues of sex discrimination in its Article 1 as:

> *"any distinction, exclusion or restriction made on the basis of sex which has the effect or purpose of impairing or nullifying the recognition, enjoyment or exercise by women, irrespective of their marital status, on a basis of equality of men and women, of human rights and fundamental freedoms in the political, economic, social, cultural, civil or any other field."*

There is a general obligation upon the States to take appropriate and effective measures to prevent any kind of violence against women[8], irrespective of custom, tradition or religious considerations.[9] "Violence against women" encompasses within its ambit *traditional practices harmful to women.*[10] The CEDAW has recommended States to strengthen legislation for the protection of women against violence.[11]

Does Burqa Violate Rights of Women?: An Analysis

Arguments in Favour

Burqa Violates Right to Equality of Women

Wearing the headscarf, women become visible twice, first as members of a religious minority (the Muslim believers), second as gendered social actors (women). Women wearing the headscarf therefore experience double discrimination as a result of the combination of their gender and race/religion characteristics.[12] This religious symbol conforms to all elements of discriminations like '*[d]istinction, exclusion or restriction made on the basis of sex...*'[13] as it (1) distinguishes women wearing Burqa from other women; (2) it excludes them from the majority in society and lastly (3) it restricts them from enjoying human rights and fundamental freedoms in the political, economic, social, cultural, civil or any other field. Even International Judicial bodies such as European Court of Human Rights in the *Dahlab v. Switzerland* also referred to the gender dimension issue, invoking the principle of gender equality as a further justification to ask the Muslim convert teacher to remove her headscarf.[14]

Burqa Encourages Oppression of Women

Yasmin Alibhai-Brown said "[a]ll the Muslim women I know detest [the burqa] but are afraid to say so because it is a mark of disloyalty."[15] Nicholas Sarkozy, French President calls burqa a symbol of subservience and of submission.[16]

According to him burqa imprisons women behind a mesh, cut off from society, and deprived her of all identity.[17] Burqa is an enveloping outer garment worn by women for the purpose of hiding a female's body when out in public.[18] This results in loss of confidence and personal identity of women. Even this mental agony and forced environment to wear Burqa created by families are covered by the definition of violence given under Art 1 of DEVAW.[19] Muslim women are daily resisting and negotiating on two fronts: internally, with patriarchal norms and family structures in the community, and externally with prejudice coming from the non-Muslim environment.[20] This creates a fear that the Muslim women who are made to 'stubbornly stick' to their own religious traditions, end up not only compromising for good their own individual freedoms but also dragging down the slope with them for their families and the whole set of well founded principles of equality and norms of social coexistence.

Arguments in Against

Burqa Ban Infringes Right to Freedom of Speech and Expression

John Dalhuisen, Amnesty International's expert on discrimination in Europe[21] and Marek Marczynski, Amnesty International's researcher on Bosnia and Herzegovina[22] opined that prohibitions on the wearing of the full face veil violates the right to freedom of expression of identity, enshrined in basic human right treaties,[23] of those women who choose to wear a full face veil as an expression of their religious, cultural, political or personal identity or beliefs.[24] As this ban does not allow Muslim women to express themselves the way they want to in public, which makes her feel ousted from the society.

Burqa Ban Infringes Right to Freedom of Religion

"The concept of worship extends to [...] the display of symbols ... The observance and practice of religion or belief may include not only ceremonial acts but also such customs as ... the wearing of distinctive clothing or head coverings."[25] The ban on Burqa by many countries violates a human right recognized by the international community as a whole. The women are not allowed to practice and profess her religion and related practices which in turn infringes Right to Freedom of Religion. Moreover, penalizing followers of a particular religion in the name of liberating oppressed women is against the concept of secularism and social justice. In particular, most non-Muslims are prejudiced towards Muslim women wearing a veil, wrongly assuming that they are oppressed and illiterate, and without acknowledging the possibility that Muslim women could be autonomous and intelligent individuals.

Should India Follow France?

France is on its way to ban burqa in its territory. The question to be discussed is that should India follow France? And secondly is India in position to follow France?

Should India Follow France?

India is a party to CEDAW, ICCPR, and ICESCR etc. which impose a duty on the State to protect a major population from gradual deterioration. Headscarves, and by definition the Muslim women wearing them, now-a-days stand for "everything that is thought to be wrong with Islam".[26] There are obligations on India similar to those of France, to take all measures to eliminate violence and discrimination against women,[27] even if it is on the basis on traditional practices and religion.[28] The Constitution of India gives all reasonable protection to every religion and full liberty to its followers under Article 25 (1).[29] But this right is always *"subject to public order, morality and health and to the other provisions of this Part"*. This right to religion gets restricted by application of Article 15(3)[30], which empowers State to make special provisions for women and children. Therefore, India can take any measure including ban on Burqa, in order to fulfill its international obligations towards its nationals in pursuance to Constitution and towards International Community.

Is India in Position to Follow France?

This question is a decisive factor in coming to a concrete conclusion with respect to India's stand over cultural and religious clothings. India is a secular country with 13.4% Muslims of the total population[31] which constitutes only 10.3% of world's total Muslim Population.[32] Whereas France has 6% Muslims of its total population[33] which constitutes only 0.2% of world's total Muslim population.[34] This makes it practically impossible in a country with such vast diversity to enforce law against one of the major populations. Unlike India, Muslim population in France is very less and in addition most of the women do not wear burqa or any religiously influenced symbol. Moreover, it is not feasible to compare India with France due to their developmental status. India is a developing country whereas France is a developed country. India has its religious culture and practice deeply imbibed in it. Whereas France does not recognize concepts like minority, their cultural rights, their practices, etc. Therefore, this answers the moot question that India is not yet ready ban burqa, as the social, religious and political cost of banning the burqa will be greater than the liberalization of women so intended. Also such step might not be viable to implement considering the religious sentiments.

Conclusion

After the above discussion it can be concluded that burqa cannot be banned in India completely at present due to societal non acceptance. This is so even when it is one of the major reasons for the alleged under-development of this sect of society. Therefore, it can be considered against the concept of development. But at the same time it forms the part of religion of Muslims and the Constitution of India gives them right to practice and profess their religion in any manner not barred by law. The issue, however, has become a global touchstone for the nature and future of the secular state. While the signatories to the International Conventions on Human Rights are near universal and every country insists on its own model of the freedom of religion, the willingness of judges and legislators to limit those rights has become more evident due to increasing instances of discrimination and violence. Now it is only France ban on Burqa which can prove whether such a ban is acceptable in world community and to what extent. And this would ultimately decide the fate of social co-existence and social development on the earth, to make it a better place to live.

Notes

1. Edward J. Eberle "Free Exercise of Religion in Germany and the United States" 78/4 Tulane Law Review 10231088 (March 2004) as referred in Paul Morris *"Covering Islam – Burqa And Hijab: Limits To The Human Right To Religion"* Human Rights Research available at *http://www.victoria.ac.nz/nzcpl/HRRJ /vol2/Morris.pdf* as visited on 01 December, 2010 at 1140.
2. The Meaning of Holy Quran Sura 24:31 (Abdulla Yusuf Ali Trans, Aimana Publications, 10th ed. 1999)
3. Leila Ahmed "Women And Gender in Islam: Historical Roots of Modern Debate" 55 (1992).
4. *Ibid.*
5. Cheryl Bernard "French Tussle Over Muslim Head Scarf is Positive Push for Women's Right, Christian Science Monitor" (Jan 5, 2004) available at *http://www.csmonitor.com/2004/0105/p09s01-coop.html* as referred in Gregor Puppinck, et. al. "Legitimacy of the French Proposal to Ban the Burqa in Public Square" European Centre for Law and Justice (March 18, 2010) at 3.
6. Universal Declaration on Human Rights (hereinafter UDHR), Article 18; International Covenant on Civil and Political Rights (hereinafter ICCPR), Article 18.
7. UDHR Art 2; International Covenant on Economic, Social and Cultural Right Art 2.2(hereinafter ICESCR); ICCPR Art 2.
8. Declaration on the Elimination of Violence against Women [hereinafter as DEVAW], G.A. res. 48/104, 48 U.N. GAOR Supp. (No. 49) U.N. Doc. A/48/49 (1993), Art. 4; African Charter on Human and Peoples' Rights [hereinafter as Banjul Charter] , 27 June 1981, 1520 U.N.T.S. 217, art.3(4) ,4 (2)(a)and(b).
9. DEVAW, *Ibid*, art. 4.
10. *Ibid* at Art. 2(a); Banjul Charter, supra n. 8, Art. 5.
11. Committee on the Elimination of Discrimination against Women, General Recommendation No. 12, Sess. 8, (1989) at 1; Human Rights Committee, General Comment No. 28 (2000) U.N. Doc. CCPR/C/21/Rev.1/Add.10, at 22.
12. Valérie Amiraux "The Headscarf Question: What is Really the Issue?" at 137 available at *http://se2.isn. ch/serviceengine/Files/RESSpecNet/45673/ichaptersection_singledocument/6BA0681E-002F-4D6E-A166-EAE9812A2D1C/en/7_Headscarf.pdf* as visited on 23rd October, 2010 at 1200.

13. Article 1, Convention on Elimination of Discrimination against Women (hereinafter CEDAW) defines "discrimination against women".
14. *Dahlab v. Switzerland*, European Court of Human Rights, Judgment of 15 February 2001, Appl. Nr. 42393/98.
15. Yasmin Alibhai-Brown "They are Right to Ban Burqa even if it is for wrong reason" Independent (Jan 8, 2010) available at *http://www.independent.co.uk/opinion/coometators/yasmin-alibhai-brown/yasmin-alibhaibrown- they-are-right-to-ban-burqa-even-if-it-is-for-wrong-reasons-1861412.html.*
16. In historic speech, Sarkozy urges burqa ban in France - Summary, 22 Jun 2009, *http://www.earthtimes.org/articles/news/274328,in-historic-speech-sarkozy-urges-burqa-ban-in-france – summary.html#* as visited on 21 November, 2010 at 1555.
17. Sarkozy Stirs French Burka Debate, 22 Jun 2009, *http://news.bbc.co.uk/2/hi/europe/8113778.stm,* as visited on 21 November, 2010 at 1535.
18. Muslim Women Dress Code In Non-Muslim Countries, UN Human Rights Council, Study Guide as available at *http://www.zagimun.org/download/UNHRC-Study_Guide.pdf* as visited on 22nd October, 2010 at 1445.
19. Article 1 of Declaration on the Elimination of Violence against Women, General Assembly Resolution 48/104 of 20 December 1993, "the term violence against women means *any act of gender-based violence that results in, or is likely to result in, physical, sexual or psychological harm or suffering to women, including threats of such acts, coercion or arbitrary deprivation of liberty, whether occurring in public or in private life*"
20. Sara Silvestri "Unveiled Issues: Reflections from a Comparative Pilot Study on Europe's Muslim Women" Working paper on Transnational Politics, (April 2009) at 8.
21. Belgium votes to ban full-face veils, 31 April, 2010, Amnesty International available at *http://www.amnesty.org/en/news-and-updates/belgium-votes-ban-full-face-veils-2010-04-30* as visited on 21 November, 2010 at 1130.
22. Bosnia and Herzegovina must reject Burqa ban, 1 September, 2010, Amnesty International available at *http://www.amnesty.org/en/news-and-updates/bosnia-and-herzegovina-must-reject-burqa-ban-2010-09-01* as visited on 21 November, 2010 at 1135.
23. ICCPR, Art.19(3); UDHR, Art. 19.
24. Report of Asma Jahangir, Special Rapporteur on Freedom of Religion or Belief, E/CN.4/2006/5 (9 January 2006) at 36.
25. United Nations Human Rights Committee General Comment No. 22, issued to clarify the meaning of article 18 (Forty-eighth session, 1993), adopted on July 20, 1993, Doc.CCPR/C/21/Rev.1/Add.4, para 4.
26. J. Scott "Symptomatic Politics. The Banning of Islamic Headscarves in French Public Schools", *French Politics, Culture & Society*, Vol. 23, 3, (2005) pp. 106-127.
27. Art 2 CEDAW.
28. Art 2(a) DEVAW.
29. Constitution of India, Article 25(1) "...all persons are equally entitled to freedom of conscience and the right freely to profess, practice and propagate religion."

30. Constitution of India, Article 15(3) "Nothing in this article shall prevent the State from making any special provision for women and children."
31. See "Population of India by Religion" available at *http://socialjustice.nic.in/pdf/tab18.pdf* as visited on 11th November, 2010 at 1200.
32. Mapping The Global Muslim Population, A Report on the Size and Distribution of the World's Muslim Population, October 2009 by Pew Forum on Religion & Public Life available at *http://pewforum.org/newassets/images/reports/Muslimpopulation/Muslimpopulation.pdf* as visited on 12th November, 2010 at 1230.
33. *Ibid.*
34. *Ibid.*

WORKING WOMEN: PROBLEMS, STATUTES AND JUDICIAL DECISIONS

*M. S. Benjamin**

Introduction

At the global level, women participation in the labour market remain the same in the last two decades from 1990 to 2010, hovering about 52%. In contrast global labour force participation rates for men declined steadily over the same period from 81% to 77%.[1] Though there is increase in women participation rate, still their participation in the work force falls below 50%, for instance, in some sub-regions: below 30% in Northern Africa and Western states, below 50% in the Caribbean and Central America.[2] Contrary to the global perception, today women constitute a significant part of the workforce in India. They are found in highly skilled, technical, managerial and decision-making positions particularly, in professions like teaching, engineering, electronics, computer technology, medicine, legal, human relations accounts, airlines, fashion designing and many others. Women no longer are considered passive members of the society.[3] In urban India Women have impressive number in the workforce, for instance at software industry 30% of the workforce is female.[4] In rural India, agriculture and allied industrial sectors employ as much as 89.5% of the total female labour. In overall farm production, women's average contribution is estimated at 55% to 66% of the total labour[5]. According to a 1991 World Bank report, women accounted for 94% of total employment in dairy production in India. Women constitute 51% of the total employed in forest-based small-scale enterprises.[6] Industries which employ more women than men are Beedi and match manufacturing, cotton textiles, cotton spinning, cashewnut

* *Assistant Professor, Department of Law, University of Mysore, Mysore, Karnataka, South India.*

processing, tobacco stemming and redrying, canning, preserving and fish processing.[7] However, women share in employment is 30% of the total work force in India since women's work participation rate widely differs from state to state.[8]

Genesis and Growth of Labour Welfare Jurisprudence

The birth of labour legislation can be found in industrial revolution but existed in rudimentary form in our country.[9] The early legislation primarily focused on the relationship between master and servant and abolished the doctrine of 'laissez faire' on the basis of freedom of contract in the interest of labour force. The traditional right of an employer to 'hire and fire' his workmen at his will has been subjected to severe restraints.[10] The right of labour is not based on the 'bargaining power', rather, on the 'status'.[11] As a result of industrialization, the gap between the rich and the poor developed such an extent that created distinct classes in industrial society i.e., 'haves' and 'have nots'. The economic disparity leads to struggle between 'haves' and 'have nots', the latter exploited.[12] The workmen realized the importance of unity and fight together against their exploitation by the rich employers. With the rise of cost of living, there has been consistent demand for increase in wages and provide some working facilities. The emergence of Democratic philosophies and values cannot be ignored along the industrial revolution. There came to be recognized certain principles which are regarded as basic, fundamental and human rights in almost all over the industrial world. These principles are...

(a) The right of workmen to establish and maintain trade unions;

(b) The change of economic philosophy from the laissez faire to a welfare state;

(c) Settlement of disputes between workmen and employer with the involvement of the government concerned;

(d) The role of the state as a protector of the marginalized section of the public;

(e) Evolving welfare policies and programmers for the welfare of workers.[13]

In spite of labour policies adopted by the government[14] and the support of courts for the cause of labour, a vast number of the people who in their relation with the employer still continued to be governed by the doctrine of laissez faire and the concept of social justice finds no place in the working force. Because workers were illiterate and gullible, therefore, unconscious of their rights, socio-economic status of the workers was far below the status of their employer. As such they could not exercise their free will in negotiating with the employer for employment. The employer taking advantage of the poor condition of the workers dictated their own terms and conditions with regard to wages, hours of work, leave etc.[15] since the labour problems were viewed as a serious menace to the society, a number of legislations were passed to regulate the recruitment and protect the interest of the workers.[16] However, these legislative measures introduced prior to Independence did not take into consideration the interest of women workers in the industry and failed to meet the socio-economic needs of the larger number of women of our country. To some extent, there could be amelioration of workers in general but so far as women workers are concerned, the concept of social security and equality had been totally ignored by the government.

After attaining independence, the government ventured into enact series of legislations for promoting welfare of women employees in conformed to the Constitution of India and International Labour Organization Conventions and Recommendations.[17] These legislations mandate for providing minimum wages, washing facilities, facilities for storing and drying clothing, facilities for sitting, canteens, shelters, rest rooms and lunch rooms, crèches, wages during leave period, weekly day of rest, maternity benefit, prohibition on employment of women in hazardous occupation and night shift etc.

Merely because there exist labour welfare legislations and policies and the Constitution provides for equality between men and women[18], equal opportunity[19], equal pay for equal work[20], just and human conditions of work[21], special provision for women[22] renounces practices of derogatory to the dignity of women[23] and prohibition of discrimination of any sort[24], it doesn't mean that women's work are considered to be at par with men's work and the efficiency and performance of women has been duly recognized and encouraged positively.

The present article brings into light the real problems faced by women in the workforce and how the judiciary tries to solve such problems using the constitution of India, statutes and international conventions and treaties as an instrument of ensuring equality and safety of women.

Inequality at Work

Article 14 mandates for equality before the law and equal protection of the laws[25]. The rule of equality cannot be understood in its absolute sense; rather, it is to be considered in the context of Aristotelian's rule of equality, in other words, like should be treated alike. All persons who are similarly situated shall be treated alike both in respect of privileges conferred and liabilities imposed.[26] Article 14 prohibits discrimination between persons who are substantially in similar circumstances[27] and it does not forbid different treatment among unequals.[28] Classification is also permissible on two conditions such as it must be founded on an intelligible differentia which distinguishes persons or things that are grouped together from others left out of the group, and the differentia must have a rational relation to the object sought to be achieved by the statute in question.[29] Treating unequals as equal is as bad as unequal treatment of equals.[30] In a famous case of *E.P. Royappa v. State of Tamil Nadu* the Supreme

Court observed that the equality guarantee under article 14 is a dynamic principle and is a guarantee against arbitrariness.[31] By this provision the State could protect the interest of women employees. In *R. Vasantha v. Union of India*, exercising power conferred by section 66 of the Factories Act 1948, the respondent prohibited women from working in the night shift.[32] The petitioner contended that since she could not work between the hours of 6 a.m. to 7 a.m. She should be shifted to work at night. Such restriction would come in the way of liberation of women's rights both socio and economic and it is an impediment in their emancipation.[33] The court has held that prohibition of women's work in night has violated Article 14 of the Constitution and consequently, removed the ban. Men and women might be physically different, but it doesn't mean they are unequal.[34]

An important question as to the liability of employers to provide safe transport facility for women working in night shift arose for the consideration of the Supreme Court in *Som Mittal v. Government of Karnataka*,[35] The petitioner was the managing director of a company, in which women were employed to work at night. An employee of the company died while traveling on the night shift. Cognizance of offence was taken against the petitioner by the metropolitan magistrate under the provisions of the Karnataka Shops and Establishment Act, 1961. The petitioner filed a petition against the complaint in the High Court. However, the court declined to quash the proceedings. The appellant challenged the decision of the High Court in the Supreme Court and cited section 3(h), of the Act which exempts a person in management. The Supreme Court dismissed the appeal against the order of the High Court[36].

In *Lena Khan v. Union of India*, a regulation of Air India provides for retirement of air hostesses employed in India at the age 35 years with extension to age 45, whereas air hostesses employed outside India retire at the age of 45 as it compatible with the domestic law of England. The regulation was challenged under Article 14 of the Constitution. This case reflects the discrimination between working women in matter relating to superannuation age. The Supreme Court held that such a classification is arbitrary and cannot hold water on the ground that it complies with the domestic law of England.[37] In *Indian Hotel and Restaurants Associations v. State of Maharashtra*, the court opined that a provision which prohibits dance in bar, permit rooms and eating houses violates equality clause.[38] Section 33-A of the Bombay Police Act 1951 and Amendment Act of 2005 which bans all types of dance in bar, permit rooms and eating houses (prohibited establishments) is void. Women can dance not only in prohibited establishment but elsewhere. Considering that the object of the Legislation is to prevent dances which are obscene, vulgar or immoral and hence derogatory to the dignity of women and to prevent exploitation of women, the court observed that there is no nexus between the classification and the object of the Act[39]. If women other than as dancers can work in the prohibited establishments and that does not amount to exploitation, why when women dance to earn their livelihood, it becomes exploitation. Section 33A and consequently Section 33B are void.[40]

The Supreme Court in *Anuj Garg v. Hotel Association of India,* held that prohibiting employment of women in any part of premises in which liquor or intoxicating drug is consumed by the public results in a an invidious discrimination.[41] The court further observed that: "instead of prohibiting women employment in the bars altogether the state should focus on factoring in ways through which unequal consequences of sex differences can be eliminated. It is state's duty to ensure circumstances of safety which inspire confidence in women to discharge the duty freely in accordance to the requirements of the profession they choose to follow. Any other policy inference (such as the one embodied under section 30)[42] from societal conditions would be oppressive on the women and against the privacy rights"[43].

Discrimination in Pay

Equal pay for equal work is contained in part IV of the Constitution.[44] It intends to eradicate inequality between men and women in respect of pay for identical work. Equal pay for equal work has also been embodied in Article 7 of the International Covenant on Economic, Social, and Cultural Rights 1966.[45] The principle of equal pay or payment for equal work is basic principle of the American free enterprise system[46]. Demands for government action for equal pay for equal work began as early as 1868, when the Labour Convention in Philadelphia passed a resolution urging Federal and State Governments to pass laws securing equal salaries for equal work to all women employed under the various departments of government.[47] The General Conference of the International Labour Organisation(ILO) adopted on 29th June, 1951 the Convention Concerning Equal Remuneration for Men and Women Workers for Work of Equal Value and India is one of the signatories to the Convention.[48] However, in India, it is to be noted that equal pay for equal work is not declared as a fundamental right; rather, it is one of the Directive Principles of State Policy, yet, obligates the State to ensure that social justice is done to women. Discrimination between men and women who are substantially situated shall constitute the denial of socio-economic justice to women. There is no justification for paying less salary because of women's physical weakness. "What a man can do, a woman can do better".[49] Equal pay for equal work is not mere a dogmatic slogan or an equitable principle[50], but it is a constitutional goal to be achieved through constitutional remedies under Articles 32 and 226 of the Constitution.[51]

In *Randhir Singh v. Union of India*[52] the Supreme Court observed that although the rule of equal pay for equal work is not expressly declared as fundamental rights but is deducible from Articles 14, 16 and 39(c)[53] of the Constitution. This right is enforceable where there is unequal pay scale based on irrational classification. This rule invalidates the difference of payment between the permanent and temporary employees or even regular and casual employees so long as they perform similar work.[54] But workers working different capacity or establishment cannot automatically claim parity of payment.[55] Thus, 'equal pay for equal work' does not mean that all the members of a cadre must receive the same pay packet, irrespective of their seniority, source of recruitment, educational qualifications and various other incidents of service.[56]

In order to give effect to Article 39(d) of the Constitution and the rule of 'equal remuneration for equal work of equal value' a directive as laid down in ILO Equal Remuneration Convention 1951, the *Equal Remuneration Act, 1976* was enacted.[57] The said Act provides for the payment of equal remuneration to men and women workers[58] and for prevention of discrimination, on the ground of sex, against women in the matter of employment[59]. It ensures protection against discrimination in recruitment and promotion of men and women. It provides for the establishment of Advisory Committees to promote employment opportunities for women.[60] The Act applies to an extensive range of classes of employment list in the Schedule, which includes the informal sector. The provisions of the Act have been extended to plantations, agriculture, mines, and construction industry etc. This Act also imposes duty upon the contractor to ensure equal pay for equal work irrespective of sex.[61]

In the case of *P. Savitha v. Union of India* the respondent provided different pay scale to senior draftsmen including women draftsmen working in the Ministry of Defence. When it was challenged as violation of Article 14, the court directed the government to pay equally for equal work to all draftsmen and women. Further, it observed that where all relevant considerations are the same, that is men and women employees holding identical posts and discharging similar duties should be treated equally.[62] Similarly, in *Mackinnon Mackenzie & Co. Ltd. V. Andrey D'Costa,* the court had come across the issue in which men and women were treated differently in matter relating to payment of remuneration for the work or work of similar nature and for this the court held that the female stenographers and male stenographers working in the company are entitled to the equal remuneration for doing the same work or work of similar nature, and directed the management of the company to pay equal remuneration all the stenographers irrespective of their sex[63]. The court rejected the plea of the management that difference in remuneration is due to contract entered into with the employees by holding that the applicability of the Act does not depend upon the financial ability of the management of pay equal remuneration as provided by it.[64]

Unreasonable Restrictions

Working women are not only facing inequality or differentiation in pay scale, but forced to comply with restrictions which are not reasonable in terms of the constitution, say for instance, early retirement, prohibition on marriage, consent of husband to seek transfer or change of place of job and like.

(a) *Prohibition of marriage*: In *International Franchise Company*,[65] a service rule prohibits working women from marriage, if they want to continue to be in service. The impugned rule was struck down by the court which remarked that such rule was inconsistent with the constitution which provided for social justice. The court while declaring the rule as arbitrary and void said: "we are not impressed by these reasons for retaining a rule of this kind. Nor do we think that because the work has to be done as a team it cannot be done by married woman. We also feel that there is nothing to show that married women would necessarily be more likely to be absent than unmarried women or widows."[66]

(b) *Retirement on first pregnancy*: In the famous case of *Air Hostess*[67] while examining the constitutional validity of service regulatións which required an air hostess to retire on her first pregnancy or at the age of 35 with extension to 45 at the discretion of the Managing Director, the court observed: " the termination of the services of an air hostess under such circumstances is not only a callous and cruel act but an open insult to Indian womanhood-the most sacrosanct and cherished institution. We are constrained to observe that such a course of action is extremely detestable and abhorrent to the notions of a civilized society."[68]

(c) *Lower age of retirement:* In *Air India Cabin Crew Association v. Yeshawinee Merchant and Others*, the Supreme Court observed that fixing of lower age of retirement than males because the nature and performance of duties as electricity worker was offending Articles 14, 15 and 16 of the Constitution.[69]

Sexual Harassment at Working Place

Until 1980s no attempt has been made to evolve any measures to counter the problem of sexual harassment of women in general and women workers in particular. For the first time in 1980, US set up the American Equal Employment Opportunity Commission (EEOC) along with a set of guideline dealing with sexual harassment.[70] The Commission viewed that sexual harassment amounted to infringement of title VII of the Civil Rights Act of 1964. The EEOC guidelines define what constitutes 'sexual harassment'[71] and laid down parameters to be considered in determining whether the alleged conduct amounts to sexual harassment.[72]

In U.K. the courts have held sexual harassment to be a conduct prohibited by the Sex discrimination Act, 1975. However, the term 'sexual harassment' is not found in the 1975 Act; nor is such conduct expressly dealt with therein.[73] According to United Nations Recommendation sexual harassment is a form of gender-based violence. It is gender based because it is directed against a woman because she is a woman.[74] Like U.K. in India as there is no statutory definition, the court has defined 'sexual harassment' relying on international conventions and norms, especially the CEDAW. The court has issued certain guidelines in *Vishaka v. State of Rajasthan*[75] after taking into consideration that the present civil and penal laws in the country do not adequately provide for specific protection of women from sexual harassment at places of work and that enactment of such legislation would take a considerable time.[76]

(a) Employees or persons in charge of work place whether in public or private sector should take appropriate steps to prevent sexual harassment.

(b) Criminal proceedings to be taken immediately and special care should be taken in giving protection to the victim and witnesses.

(c) Appropriate disciplinary action should be initiated by the employer in accordance with those rules.

(d) Appropriate mechanism should be created in the employer's organization for redress of the complaint made the victim.

(e) A complaint committee should be made and to be maintained confidentially. The committee should be headed by a woman and not less than half of its members should be women.

(f) The Complaint Committee must submit its Annual Report to the Government Department concerned of the complaints and action taken by them.

(g) Employees should be allowed to raise issues of sexual harassment at workers meeting and in others appropriate forum.

(h) Rights of female employees in this regard should be notified on the prominent place of the premises.

(i) Where sexual harassment occurs, the employer or person in charge will take all steps necessary and reasonable to assist the affected person in terms of support and preventive action.

(j) The Centre/State Government should ensure that the guidelines laid down by this order are also observed by the employers in Private Sector.

However, the aforesaid rights will not prejudice any rights available under the Protection of Human Rights Act, 1993.[77]

In *Apparel Export Promotion Council v. A.K. Chopra*, the court held that any action or gesture, whether direct or by implication, aims at or has the tendency to outrage the modesty of a female employee, must fall under the general concept of the definition of sexual harassment.[78] In *Saudi Arabian Airlines, Mumbai v. Shehnaz Mudbhatkal*,[79] the victim who was a lady persisted by the Station Manager to take lunch with him and quarrying about the method of family planning adopted by her. The victim was denied promotion due to her and asked to meet him at his residence in the night to discuss the issue of her promotion. Finally, the victim was terminated from the service which appeared predated and intended to render ineffective her representation to the higher authorities. The court concluded that the victim had been sexually harassed by the officer and also victimized for not yielding to the officer's improper sexual advances by dismissal from service on false and trumped up allegations[80].

The Supreme Court in *Neera Mathur v. L.I.C.*,[81] observed that any question to a female candidate concerning personal problems such as pregnancy and menstruation whereby modesty and self-respect may preclude the disclosure of, should be deleted from enquiry by the employer. Discrimination on the ground of pregnancy can be regarded as harassment.[82]

Loss of Maternity Leave

In *Municipal Corporation of Delhi v. Female Workers (Muster Roll) and Another*, female workers engaged by the respondent-corporation raised a demand for grant of maternity leave which was made only to regular female workers but was denied to them on the ground that their services were not regularized and therefore they were not entitled to any maternity leave. Relying on Articles 39 and 42 the Supreme Court held that the Maternity Benefit Act 1961 did not say that only regular women employees entitled the benefit of maternity leave and not those who are engaged on casual basis or on muster roll on daily wage basis. Women who constitute almost half of the segment of our society have to be honored and treated with dignity at places where they work to earn their livelihood. Whatever be the nature of their duties their avocation and the place where they work they must be provided all the facilities to which they entitled. The court further held that the principles contained in Article 11 of CEDAW have to be read into the contract of service between the respondent corporation and the women employees and so read these employees immediately become entitled to all the benefits conceived under the Maternity Benefit Act, 1961.[83]

Conclusion

In the contemporary world, women are not inferior or incompetent in terms of profession. They work hard at the workplace as well as at home. Working women refers to women who are employed for remuneration. In this context, working women may be classified into two classes, women working in the organized sector and women working in the unorganized sector. Roughly speaking, about 90 per cent of the working women are working in informal and unorganized sector, whereas only 10 per cent work in formal sector. There is no field in which women are not employed. There are several pieces of legislative policies and enactments for the protection and promotion of the interest of working women. The judiciary has also adopted pro-woman approach whenever it comes across the issue of women in relation to men. Nonetheless, working women are facing problems because of their sex. The legislative policies and measures have not achieved the object which ought to have been. The reason is the lack of competent mechanism to implement the existing labour legislations, policies and judicial dictums. Working women constitute major part of labour market in India and across the world. Their problems cannot be solved by statutes, policies and decisions; in the same breadth what is equally important is the proper implementation. In order to eliminate inequality in the workforce, discrimination in pay scale and prevent sexual harassment, there is need to constitute an ombudsman institution which will exclusively monitor the implementation of laws, policies and decisions relating to working women. The institution like ombudsman may work towards ensuring fundamental rights of equality of sexes, of right to life and liberty and of the right to practice any profession or to carry on any trade or business or right to work with dignity which is a basic human right.

Notes

1. *www.unstat.un.org/world/worker/2010.*
2. *Ibid.*
3. Mediratta, Surinder Handbook of Law, Women and Employment: Policies, Issues, Legislation and Case Law, Oxford University Press (2009) first edition, p. 12.
4. Singh, S. & Hoge, G. (2010), Debating Outcomes for 'Working' Women–Illustration from India, *The Journal of Poverty*, 14 (2), 197-215.
5. Census of India 2001.
6. *"Asia's women in agriculture, environment and rural production: India". http://www.fao.org/sd/wpdirect/WPre0108.htm.*
7. CSO, 1995.
8. 2nd National Commission on Labour 2002.
9. Mishra S.N. Labour and Industrial Laws, Central Law publications, 25th edition 2009, p. 1.
10. *Ibid.*
11. Chandra, Mahesh Industrial Jurisprudence,Tripati Private Limited, 1976, p. 40.
12. Supra note 9, p. 2.
13. Supra note 9.
14. Adopting the Code of Discipline in industry, conducting annual labour conferences, establishment of labour committees, allowing workers participation in management, promoting workers education, banning strikes and lockout without notice, providing bonus on the basis of profits or production etc.
15. Giri, V.V. Labour Problems in Indian Industry, Asia Publishing House, 1956 p. 115.
16. The Factories Act 1881, Mines Act 1901, Trade union Act of 1926, Workmen Compensation Act 1923, Payment of Wages Act 1936.
17. The Factories Act 1948; Maternity Benefit Act 1961; Equal Remuneration Act 1976; Medical Termination of Pregnancy Act 1971; Contract Labour (Regulation and Abolition) Act, 1970; Beedi and Cigar Workers' (Conditions of employment) Act 1966; Minimum Wages Act 1948; Employees State Insurance Act 1948; Employees Provident Funds Act 1952; Payment of Gratuity Act 1972; Contract Labour (Regulation and Abolition) Act, 1970; Bonded labour System (Abolition) Act 1976;

Legal Services Authorities Act, 1987; Building and Other Construction Workmen (Regulation of Employment and Conditions of Service) Act, 1996.

18. Article 14. Equality before law-"the State shall not deny to any person equality before the law or the equal protection of the laws within the territory of India."
19. Article 16. Equality of opportunity in matters of public employment.-(1) there shall be equality of opportunity for all citizens in matters relating to employment or appointment to any office under the state.....
20. Article 39(d). that there is equal pay for equal work for both men and women;
21. Article 42. Provision for just and humane conditions of work and maternity relief. The State shall make provision for securing just and humane conditions of work and for maternity relief.
22. Article 15(3). Nothing in this article shall prevent the State from making any special provision for women and children.
23. Article 51-A(e).
24. Article 15(1). The State shall not discriminate against any citizen on grounds only of religion, race, caste, sex, place of birth or any of them.
25. See Art. 14 of the Constitution of India.
26. Satish Chandra vs Union of India AIR 1953 SC 250.
27. Kathi Ranning Rawat v. State of saurashtra, AIR1 1952 SC 123.
28. Shukla V.N. Constitution of India, Eastern Book Company, 10th edition 2001, reprinted 2009 page 38.
29. The test was clearly expressed by Das J. in state of West Bengal v. Anwar Ali Sarkar, AIR 1952 SC 75.
30. All India Sainik Schools Employees Association v. Sainik Schools Society 1989 Supp. (1) SCC 205.
31. (1974) 4 SCC 3. Also see Maneka Gandhi v. Union of India, 1978 (1) SCC 248.
32. Section 66(1)(b) : no woman shall be 2[required or allowed to work in any factory] except between the hours of 6 A. M. and 7 P. M. Provided that the State Government may, by notification in the Official Gazette, in respect of 2[any factory or group or class or description of factories,] vary the limits laid down in clause (b), but so that no such variation shall authorize the employment of any woman between the hours of 10 P. M. and 5 A. M.
33. The petitioner relied on Articles 15, 16, 19(1)(g) as well as 21 of the Constitution. *www.indiankanoon.org/doc/715470/*
34. (2001) II LLJ 843 (Mad). Also see Central Railway Workshop, Jhansi v. Vishwanath AIR 1970 SC 400.
35. 2008 (3) SCC 753.
36. *Ibid.*
37. AIR 1987 SC 1515.
38. Section 33-A of the Bombay Police Act 1951: Notwithstanding anything contained in this Act or the rules made by the Commissioner of Police or the District Magistrate under sub-section (1) of Section 33 for the area under their respective charges, on

and from the date of commencement of the Bombay Police (Amendment) Act, 2005,-

(a) holding of a performance of dance, of any kind or type, in any eating house, permit room or beer bar is prohibited;

(b) all performance licences, issued under the aforesaid rules by the Commissioner of Police or the District Magistrate or any other officer, as the case may be, being the Licensing Authority, to hold a dance performance, of any kind or type, in an eating house, performance, of any kind or type, in an eating house, permit room or beer bar shall stand cancelled.

39. 2006 (3) Bom CR 705; AIR 2006 NOC 901 Bam.) 297.

40. 33B. Subject to the other provisions of this Act, or any other law for the time being in force, nothing in section 33A shall apply to the holding of a dance performance in a drama theatre, cinema theatre and auditorium; or sports club or gymkhana, where entry is restricted to its members only, or a three starred or above hotel or in any other establishment or class of establishments, which, having regard to (a) the tourism policy of the Central or State Government for promoting the tourism activities in the State; or (b) cultural activities, the State Government may, by special or general order, specify in this behalf.

Explanation: For the purposes of this section, "sports club" or "gymkhana" means an establishment registered as such under the provisions of the Bombay Public Trusts Act, 1950, or the Societies Registration Act, 1860 or the Companies Act, 1956, or any other law for the time being in force.

41. AIR 2008 SC 663.

42. Section 30 of the Punjab Excise Act, 1941, prohibits employment of any woman in any part os such premises in which liquor or intoxicating drug is consumed by the public.

43. Supra note 41 at para 41. *Visit /www.indiankanoon.org/doc/845216/*

44. Supra note 20.

45. Article 7 (a) (i): Fair wages and equal remuneration for work of equal value without distinction of any kind, in particular women being guaranteed conditions of work not inferior to those enjoyed by men, with equal pay for equal work;

46. Surinder, Mediratta Handbook of Law, Women, and Employment; Policies, Issues, Legislation and Case Law, Oxford University Press 2009 at page 37.

47. L.C. Dhingra and Arvinder Singh Dalal, 'Equal pay for Equal Work and the Law; A Critical analysis', MDU Law Journal 6(1), June 2001, p.37. as cited in note 46.

48. Charu Walikhanna and Nandita Rao (ed, Supreme Court and High Court Judgments Relating to Women and Children, (2005), Serials Publications, first edition at p. 42.

49. See National Commission for Women, Annual Report 2000-2001, p. 200.

50. State of Maharashtra v. Association of Court Stenos and Other, AIR 2002 SC 591.

51. See Surendar Singh v. Engineer in Chief P.W.D., AIR 1986 SC 584.

52. AIR 1982 SC 879. Also see Jeet Singh v. MCD 1986 Supp SCC 560; Delhi Veterinary Assn v. Union of India, (1984) 3 SCC 1.

53. Article 39 (c). That the operation of economic system does not result in the concentration of wealth and means of production to the common detriment.
54. Jaipal v. State of Haryana (1988) 3 SCC 3354.
55. Assam Sillimanite Limited v. Union of India, 1992 Supp (1) SCC 692 ; AIR 1992 SC 938.
56. State of A.P. and Others v. G. Sreenivasa Rao & others (1989) II L.L.J. 149 (SC). It was held in Government of West Bengal v. Tarun K. Roy,(2004) I L.L.J. 421 (SC), that the principle of equal pay for equal work would not apply where educational qualifications and other considerations such as source of recruitment and nature of work done vary between two classes of employees, although nature of work done is the same.
57. The President of India promulgated on 26th September, 1975, the Equal Remuneration Ordinance, 1975 so that article 39(d) could be implemented in the year which was being celebrated as the International Women's year.
58. Section 4 of the Equal Remuneration Act 1976.
59. Section 5 of the Act 1976.
60. Section 6 of the Act 1976.
61. See section 16(b) of the Act 1976.
62.
63. AIR 1987 SC 1281.
64. *Ibid.* Aslo see Smt. Bimla Rani w/o Padam Bhadur and Others v. appellate Authroity equal Remuneration Act, 1976, the Co operative Store Ltd., through its general Manager, Dr. A.K. Mishra, official liquidator, The Co operative Store Ltd. And the Central Registrar, Multi State Co operative Socieities, MANU/DE/0630/2004.
65. AIR 1966 SC 942.
66. Ibid at page 944.
67. Air India v. Nargesh Meerza AIR 1981 SC 1829.
68. *Ibid* at page 1850.
69. AIR 2004 SC 187.
70. Equal Employment Opportunity Commission (EEOC), guidelines on Discrimination Because of Sex, 29 CFR 1604. 11 (a) (1985).
71. It includes unwelcome sexual advances, requests for sexual favours, and other verbal or physical conduct of a sexual nature constitute sexual harassment when (a) submission to such conduct is made either explicitly or implicitly a term or condition of an individual's employment (b) submission to or rejection of such conduct by an individual is used as the basis for employment decisions affecting such individual, or (c) such conduct has the purpose or effect of unreasonably interfering with an individual's work performance or creating an intimidating, hostile, or offensive working environment.
72. Basin, Alok Sexual Harassment at Work, Eastern Book Company, first edition 2007, at page 11.
73. *Ibid* page 12.

74. See the Committee on the elimination of Discrimination against Women constituted by the United Nations in its General Recommendation No. 19 January 1992. The recommendation defined the term 'sexual harassment' as "sexual harassment includes such unwelcome sexually determined behavior as physical contacts and advances, sexually coloured remarks showing pornography and sexual demands, whether by worlds or actions. Such conduct can be humiliating and constitute a health and safety problem; in its discriminatory when the woman has reasonable grounds to belief that her objection would disadvantage her in connection with employment including recruiting or promotion, or when it creates a hostile working environment. Document No. CEDAW/1992/L/Add. 15.

75. AIR 1997 SC 3011; (1997) 6 SCC 241, a Sathin in the government-run Women's Development Programme, was raped during the course of her work of pre venting child marriage in Rajasthan. The writ petition was filed for the enforcement of fundamental rights of working women under Articles 14, 19 and 21 of the Constitution which guarantees the right to equality, life, and liberty to all citizens.

76. Munish, Gandhi (compiled) Justice for Women Concerns and Expressions by Dr. justice A.S. Anand, Universal Law Publishing co. Pvt. Ltd. First edition 2002 at p. 227.

77. Saharay, Madhusudan (ed) Public Interest Litigation and human Rights in India, first edition 2000, Premier publishing Company at page 117.

78. AIR 1999 SC 625, while a female employee was a subordinate, the respondent was the superior officer in the Apparel Export Promotion Council. Although she was not qualified to take dictation from the respondent, with an ulterior motive, respondent forced her to accompanying him to Taj Hotel where he intended to give dictation. In that hotel, respondent attempted to molest in spite of her protest.

79. (1999)2 LLJ 109 (Bom).

80. *Ibid.*

81. (1992) 1 SCC 286.

82. In Italy a job candidate who is pregnant is protected by the equal rights law which prohibits "any and all discrimination at the time of taking on based on the sex of the job candidate and any and all discrimination related to a woman's state of pregnancy". In France a clause in the 1975 maternity protection law, which is a part of the employment legislation, prohibits employers from seeking information from a job candidate regarding pregnancy: being pregnant must not be an obstacle to taking on. There is no policy in the UK that deals specifically with the protection of prospective employees who are pregnant at the time of taking on. European Journal of Public Health 1993; 3: 48-53. Also visit *www.oxfordjournals.org*.

83. (2000) 3 SCC 224.

TRANSITION FROM JOINT FAMILY TO NUCLEAR FAMILY AND ELDERLY CONCERNS

*Binusha Joie**

Introduction

In today's world, joint families are pictures of the past. Nuclear families have become trendy and almost everyone seems to be following the trend. People don't have the time to share the joys and sorrows of their very own kith and kin. They move off to live in a world of their own. This reduces the love they experience as well as their ability to love others. They have time only for themselves. Their work, immediate family members and the very few activities done for the sake of providing themselves entertainment restrict their thoughts, imagination and expression of emotions. The working people or the youngster's of nuclear families may find it very convenient, but there are people who suffer due to this. They are the elders in the family. They suffer due to their way of living for the past years of life. Their small world would have revolved around their large families. A joint family would have been what they had lived all their life. When every family in the joint family decides to form nuclear families, the ones who suffer are the elders, the ones who had been the pillars of the family all the while it was young and till the family was standing on its feet. Once everyone moves out to form smaller families, they get left out with nowhere to go, no one to care for them and no one to share their feelings and problems with. The transition from joint families to nuclear families is a major source of concern for the elders. By taking a look into the lives of elders who had to live alone or with a nuclear family, studies of the problems they face have been made. These problems make them everything from unhappy to mentally unstable.

---

* *B.Sc. Psychology, Student, III year, B.Sc Psychology, PSG College of Arts & Science, Peelamedu, Coimbatore, Tamilnadu, (binushajoie@hotmail.com)*

Method

Direct interaction with the individuals who have undergone the transition from joint family to nuclear family and have gone through many problems due to that has been followed. By looking into their world from their view, it has been easier to understand and come to know of their problems. Discussed below are the problems they face.

Results

The concerns of elders who undergo transition from joint family to nuclear family are many. They have difficulty in expressing their thoughts and emotions due to their age and mentality. But once they understand that they have understood that there is someone they can confide in, they have a lot to tell, including their problems, life experiences and about the ones they care for.

Types	*Males*		*Females*
Elders already undergone the transition	4		4
Elders in joint families	1		2
Elders in nuclear families for long period	2		2
Total		15	

The following has been discussed based on the study conducted on a total of 15 elderly people of various socio-economic classes as well as different cultural groups.

Discussion

Facing Loneliness

The scenarios in joint families are completely different from those of nuclear families. There is someone or the other with everyone all the time. People hardly feel lonely in joint families. They share their lives with all their siblings, children and their parents. They experience a lot of love and warmth in joint families. This is something that can not be matched by any other love and warmth. Each member's problem or happiness becomes a problem or happiness for the entire family. Even leisure times are spent with everyone else in fun activates or just chatting away about the days happenings.

But when the elderly are put in a nuclear family, their narrow mindset makes it difficult for them to face the fact that they now have to live with very few people. Loneliness is the main problem that these elderly ones experience. The feeling that they are now no longer with so many people who loved them brings down their liveliness. The kind of loneliness they experience is something that they cannot describe. At their age and because of their mentality, they are totally unable to explain how they feel but can only cry, shrug shoulders, or make faces which speak for how they feel. The feeling of loneliness is the root cause of all the other concerns that they have. For them their world will have narrowed down to the very few people who they see sometimes, and become very empty. The warmth of each member in the joint family is missed greatly in the nuclear family. The memories of incidents that took place and the moments of happiness that they shared as a joint family will be the only things keeping them company in their loneliness. This makes them long all the more for those moments again, making their loneliness more profound. This loneliness makes them pull away from other activities and from gatherings. They begin to assume reasons for which they have become lonely. They consider themselves guilty for small reasons which they feel would have hurt the ones who have moved away from them. These thoughts make them feel that they have been the reason for their loneliness. Had not loneliness been a problem, most of the following problems would not have existed.

Loss of Emotional Support

At home in a joint family, every member shares his/her life with the rest of the family. The joys and sorrows of each member become the joys and sorrows of the entire house. During any time of crisis the elders who have to take responsibility, are emotionally supported by everyone else at home. The burdens of the problems are shared by everyone and so the weight of the actual problem on the elders is reduced. During times of loss of loved ones or anything of great value to the family, the elders who are most greatly affected are supported by the rest of the family. This reduces the pain and stress they have to go through. By sharing the problems with the rest of the family, they feel greatly relieved. The emotional support they receive from the family too helps them get over the problems faster, and also makes them more easily relieved. This in turn helps them think logically enough so as to find solutions to the problem. The children of joint families are usually not much affected during times of loss of a relative, as the elders are. At this time, the elders receive valuable emotional support from the rest of the family. The intensity of the grief is lessened with this comfort.

In a nuclear family, the elders usually do not have anyone to talk to or share their problems with, either they are alone and the only one they have to share their problems and feelings with may be their partner who is also elderly and may not be able to provide as much emotional support as a large family would be. Or they may be part of a nuclear family of which now-a-days the members are usually working and so do not have time to share the problems of the elders. These people may not have the patience to understand the grief and sorrow the elders experience and so do not even try to comfort them in any way. This leaves the elders to bear all the emotional problems by themselves. the feeling that they have no one to give them emotional support tires them emotionally making them prone to tears at the slightest provocation not only does the entire weight of their grief rest on them but also the sorrow that they now no longer have no one to support them emotionally heightens their sorrow.

No One to Share their Feelings

Emotions play a big role in every person's life. As emotions brew up, the more they are shared with others the easier it becomes to deal with them. Every emotion has its own effect on the person who experiences it. In a joint family, people are more open to sharing their feelings with others. Even if they try to hide their feelings someone or the other will be able to make out what has upset them. Happy feelings are shared with the rest of the family and this multiplies the happiness. Youngsters and working people are able to overcome or suppress emotions since they may have a lot to do and more of support from the society that they associate with. Elders tend to have few associates and so chances of having people close enough to them for them to share their feelings with are few. In a joint family the elders are sometimes comfortable to share their feelings with atleast a few in the family whereas they are not equally comfortable with their associates. The feeling that if not one person there is always another person with who they can share their feelings is also a source of comfort when confronted with problems. This is the positive side of being in a joint family.

When the elders are living alone as a result of others having moved away to form nuclear families, they have no one to share their feelings with except their partners, but this may not always be their best option. They have not much to do and so find it harder to suppress or overcome their feelings. When these elders live with a nuclear family, they sometimes try to hide their feelings so as to not let it show out or not to burden the family they stay with. Also they feel that expressing their feelings may seem like a sign of their weakness. The people in the nuclear family do not have time for the feelings of elders and also consider their feelings as unnecessary emotions. All this stops elders from sharing their feelings with anyone. Keeping their feelings to themselves create tension in them and also increase the feeling in them that they now have no one for them. The elders, as a result of not being able to share their feelings, grow more disturbed and are unable to think clearly or solve their problems by themselves. Feelings which were kept shut out from the world were what disturbed elders the most and this made them the hardest to understand.

Feel Less Secure

The security which a large family provides is definitely not comparable with anything else. No security officer or commando team can provide the same feeling of safety a large family can. Elders lived in this sort of families all their lives. Even without their knowledge they would have had the sense of security within their family that they never experienced elsewhere. It would automatically be in the corner of their mind that for anything and everything they had people who they could rely on around them all the time. This not only boosts their confidence, but also makes them have a firmer stand in whatever they did. Being with many members made it easier to share the responsibility of keeping each member safe with everyone else. The whole scenario changes when they have to live in nuclear families or alone. They have no support with them. No one to stand by their side during times of trouble. This makes them feel less secure, making them less confident about their abilities. Doubt arises in them as to what they can do by themselves, which may surprisingly be the same things that they used to do all by themselves when they were with their large families. This may make them dependent on others around them or may stop them from fulfilling a necessity completely. These changes may be awkward or irritating to the family they stay with them, but only by understanding the change in mental situation of the ones suffering the major impact of the shift, can these problems be rectified.

Loss of Physical Assistance

For those elders who have been in need of assistance due to physical inabilities, the shift from a large family into a nuclear family may be a large bang. The assistance that they received from many members would have to be shared now just by a limited number of members. This may make those few members find it a burden over a time to look after the needs of the elders. When there are many members, the work could be shared among them so that it would not come to them as a burden. As a result of the constant need to assist the elder, reluctance may develop in the member of this nuclear family leading to failure in assisting the elder. This can lead to many problems including strengthening of intensity in physical problems in the individual and the emotional problems which result due to lack of care.

Moving onto smaller problems which affect the elderly during and after transition into nuclear families, these problems are usually neglected or overlooked. But the impact they have on the mind, even though small may over time lead to serious problems. This would not only affect the elderly individual but also those who associate with them.

More Time to Think About Problems

As a result of being alone for more time when they are in nuclear families, the elderly have more time to spend for themselves and their problems. Having fewer people around them at all times gives them more time for thought. Problems which they would have put aside as a result of their ever busy lifetime looking after everyone else or just being busy enjoying the company of every other member in the family, will start being the only things they have to worry about in the absence of the other members. These problems which were once small and negligible to themselves seem to become bigger and bigger and eventually tend to take over their lives. Though this may seem impossible, by observing the lives of the elderly in such situations it will not be surprising to find them complaining about small problems. They also tend to find fault with small things that happen around them. All this makes them feel that there is nothing but problems around them. This mentality makes them disturbed and anxious which as a cycle, results in more physical and emotional problems.

Psychological Disorders and Physical Illnesses

Issues which may seem least important to youngsters or to members of the nuclear family, who are busy with their lives, may not be so to the elders who have to stay in these families. To them small problems may seem very large because they have nothing else to occupy their time or worry about. Being too anxious may result in somatoform disorders or factitious disorders. Psychological disorders like depression, anxiety disorders are also common in elders who have to undergo transition from large families to nuclear families. The feeling that they now have no one around them to care for them is another factor which results in these disorders. the need for care and attention increases as age increases and when this decreases, psychological disorders and physical illnesses come up in their lives making life all the more miserable to the lonely elders.

Feeling of Inferiority/Being a Burden

Being in a family where there are lot of members and having to head the family as an elder, would have given the elders a sense of superiority. Once the family breaks down to nuclear ones, the elders loose their position as head of the family. They then have to rely on others in the family to look after their needs. This makes them feel that they are a burden to those who look after them. Not only do they feel that they are a burden, but also a sense of inferiority fills their mind. The thought that they were once independent and now are dependent on others makes them feel small and low.

Unison in Taking Decisions

For members of large families, decision making is usually not something that could be done by oneself. It was shared by almost everyone who was associated with the matter. Being the elder of a large family meant, having the largest say in the decision making of the house. Once the family is a nuclear one, the elders generally have not much say in the decision making. It is the family which takes decisions according to their convenience, sometimes even for the elderly. Even if the elders had to take some decisions, it would usually be for them only. This feeling of loss of place and stand can have a mighty effect on the mind of the elderly.

Loss of Leadership Position

In a house where a large family resided, the elder of the house was considered the head of the family. Decisions would be taken under the guidance of the elder and all activities in the house were done with their consent. This made the elder hold a position of importance in the family. After the transition into a nuclear family, the situation changes. Usually the family life is decided by the man in the family in accordance to the convenience of that family. The needs and view of the elder are not always given top priority in the case of nuclear families. In the nuclear family, the elders are generally dependant on the family with whom they stay and so they have to go according to their plans. For people who had been leading others for so long, having to listen to others in their old age may seem to hurt their prestige.

Feeling of Growing Old Faster

Being alone and having plenty of time for oneself, makes them feel that they are now growing older. This makes them think of the limitations of the age. They tend to want to settle down to living a calm and peaceful life. This sort of lifestyle, according to them will reduce their needs and also stop them from being a big burden to the ones they stay with. As they lead this sort of life, the nagging thought of their age stays in their mind, in a way, reminding them of their limits. Doing this, makes them notice the signs of aging and it has a deeper impact on their mind. Elders tend to think that they are growing older faster than they actually are.

No Work to do

For those who lived in large families, a busy life would have been a normal thing. Once settled into a nuclear life, especially for the elders of the family, they do not have much to do. Their life usually becomes monotonous. Having not many activities to do makes them unable to keep up with their past life. The energy which they used to spend on all the activities stays in them and this can make them very disturbed. Many elders who don't have much to do can be seen with illnesses, and many other problems mostly feigned by them, just to keep themselves busy.

Lack Private Space

The elderly, who lived in large family houses, would have had a space of their own, mostly because it was their own house. After moving in with a nuclear family, it is usually seen that the elderly of the house do not get enough private space. Very few are fortunate to have their own rooms or private space which would provide them a little privacy. The elderly in nuclear families usually end up having to share the space with the children of the house or may have very little space for themselves. Privacy is very important for the elderly as they need to have space for their activities and for peace of mind. The need for private space for elderly is usually not understood by the families of today.

Conclusion

Problems that the elderly face just due to the transition from large families to nuclear families are too many to be faced by them in their aged world. Though they may seem small and silly to the rest of the younger world, standing in the shoes of the elders would give us a look into the intensity of their problems. By understanding their problems or atleast doing something to reduce their problems will definitely make life much better for them in their old age.

Reference

The only reference used has been the life experiences of various elderly people who have undergone the situation of change. The elders are of different socio-economic classes, and from different cultures.

VIOLENCE AGAINST WOMEN WITH SPECIAL REFERENCE TO DOMESTIC VIOLENCE IN INDIA

*D. Pulla Rao**

Introduction

Discrimination and exploitation on the basis of gender constitutes a serious issue which effectively means that half the human race is unable to realize its potential and condemned to sub-optional standards of existence. This problem has received worldwide attention and several efforts have been made to bridge the seemingly ever-widening gap. Yet, even after years of efforts to integrate women into the mainstream development process, the effectivity of the same remains to be questioned owing to a multitude of factors which aid the continued marginalization of women. Women's access to education, health, employment and political spaces still remain distant goals in many countries of the world. One of the most serious impediments to women's development is the phenomenon of continuing and increasing violence against them. Needless to say, this constitutes a serious violation of woman's human rights. Gender violence manifests itself in various forms - female foeticide and infanticide, sexual abuse, incest, molestation, sexual harassment at work and on the streets, marital rape, domestic violence in the form of wife assault and women battering. Of all the forms of violence that women face, domestic violence remains the least reported and largely suppressed.

Violence against women is socially a very sensitive issue and more so in our country where we have a special place for 'Family Honour'. Any act which affects the family honour is not tolerated and very strongly put down. Therefore the acts of violence are seldom talked-out of the family and its close confines.

---

* *Professor of Economics, 3/5, Siripuram Quarters, Andhra University, Visakhapatnam-3, A.P.*

Violence against women is widespread and viewed as one of the cruelest social mechanisms to suppress women. Unequal power relations have led to discrimination against women. Violence on women manifests even before birth and early life, married life as domestic violence, rape, murder, dowry death etc.

The basic reason for violence against women is their inferior status educationally, economically, politically, and socially- in a male dominated society. Other factors responsible for increasing criminalization of society, media images inadequate means to address the cause and consequences of violence's; poor enforcement of legal provisions, unabashed consumerism and erosion of family values have all added to it. Over the past decade, there has been growing awareness of this phenomenon and its long-term impact on women empowerment. The media reports extensively on dowry deaths, rape, molestation, incest, assault etc. and give out information that was virtually unavailable till a few years ago.

Categories of Violence Against Woman in India

Though woman's movement has had a long history of raising various concerns, violence was not the central issue till late seventies. Around late seventies the issues like dowry, wife beating were in the forefront and through them women's concerns were expressed. Initially the measure like legal aid centres and counseling services were taken by the Government and Non-Governmental Organisations. That was the starting point. The issue of violence against woman started coming in to the forefront from early eighties onwards. The issue was widely discussed and advocated due to continuous efforts of woman's organization and activists. Very broadly, if we want to assess the situation of today, we can categorize violence against women in the following manner:

Violence within family

- Wife beating and battering
- Dowry deaths
- Sexual abuse of female children
- Incest at all stages of a woman's life
- Unwanted pregnancy
- Female foeticide and infanticide
- Alcoholism
- Impact of patriarchal values
- Domination and control within family
- Cultural reasons

Violence within community or society at large

- Sexual Harassment , molestation and intimidation at work
- Rape
- Kidnapping and abduction
- Sexual abuse
- Stripping and shaming of women
- Trafficking
- Forced prostitution
- Caste and communal violence
- Women's rights over their bodies denied
- Feminization of poverty
- commercial Interests of Sex work industry

Violence in difficult circumstances like Wars and Riots

- Rape
- Sexual harassment and abuse
- Occupation of opponents military
- War crimes

The Rise of Offences against Women

Despite existence of special legislations, providing protection to women, the proportion of crime against women as compared to the total IPC crimes has increased from 3.5 per cent in 1998 to 9.3 per cent in 2004 (Table 1).

Table 1
Crimes against Women Under IPC: 1998-2004

Year	*Total IPC Crimes*	*Crimes Against Women (IPC) Cases*	*Percentage to total IPC Crimes*
1998	1778815	119012	6.7
1999	1764629 (-0.8%)	123122 (3.5%)	7.0
2000	1771084 (0.4%)	128320 (4.2%)	7.2
001	1769308 (-0.1%)	130725 (1.9%)	7.4
2002	1780.330 (0.6%)	131112 (0.3%)	7.4
2003	1716120(-3.6%)	131364 (0.2%)	7.6
2004	1832015 (6.75%)	143615 (9.3%)	7.8

Source: GOI, Crime in India, 2001, National Crime Records Bureau, 2003 and 2005.

Incidence of Offences Against Women by Category

The data in Table 2 represents incidence of crimes committed against women during1996-2004. Torture (cruelty by husband and relatives) occupies the first place and accounts for 37.66 per cent of crimes followed by molestation which is 22.40 per cent. Both these crimes account for 55 to 60 per cent during 1996 to 2004. Rape, kidnapping and abduction cases account for 22 to 26 per cent while sexual harassment, dowry death and others account for the rest.

Of the nine categories of violence, crimes such as torture, rape, kidnapping & abduction, dowry death and others have increased in 2004 over 2003. Sexual harassment has decreased from 8.77 per cent in 2003 to 6.48 per cent in 2004 due to the intervention of government and follow up action taken to fulfill the directions of Hon'ble Supreme Court.

Andhra Pradesh (with 7.3% of population) has accounted for 12.3 per cent of total incidents of crime (18921 cases) in 2004. Uttar Pradesh (with 16.4% population), has accounted for 10.0 per cent of crime against women (115485 cases) in 2004. Six states viz., Andhra Pradesh (12.3%) Uttar Pradesh (9.9%), Rajasthan (8.5%), Maharashtra (7.9%), and West Bengal (7.2%) contribute 56 per cent of total crimes in 2004.

Domestic Violence

Domestic violence against women has become a global issue with the increase in the number of cases. The first ever international recognition of domestic violence was by the United Nations in 1993 with the adoption of the declaration of violence Against Women, The Declaration defined violence as physical, sexual

Table 2
Category-wise Incidence of Crime in India: 1996-2004

Types of crimes	*1996*	*1997*	*1998*	*1999*	*2000*	*2001*	*2002*	*2003*	*2004*	*Growth Rate (1996-2004)%*
Torture	35246	36592	41376	43823	45778	49170	49237	50703	58121	64.9
	(30.46)	(30.18)	(31.47)	(32.28)	(32.38)	(34.19)	(34.42)	(36.06)	(37.66)	
Molestation	28939	30764	30959	32311	32940	34124	33943	32939	34567	19.4
	(25.01)	(25..37)	(23.55)	(23.80)	(23.30)	(23.73)	(23.73)	(23.43)	(22.40)	
Rape	14846	15330	15151	15468	16496	16075	16373	15847	18233	22.8
	(12.83)	(12.64)	(11.52)	(11.39)	(11.67)	(11.18)	(11 45)	(11.27)	(11.81)	
Kidnapping &	14877	15617	16351	15962	15023	14645	14506	132[illegible]6	15578	4.7
Abduction	(12.85)	(12.88)	(12.44)	(11.76)	(10.63)	(10.19)	(10.14)	(9.46)	(10.09)	
Sexual	5671	5796	8054	8858	11024	9746	10.55	12325	10001	76.3
Haressment	(4.90)	(4.78)	(6.13)	(6.52)	(7.80)	(6.78)	(7.10)	(8.77)	(6.48)	
Dowry Death	5513	6006	6975	6699	6995	6851	6822	6208	7026	27.4
	(4.76)	(4.95)	(5.31)	(4.93)	(4.95)	(4.76)	(4.77)	(4.41)	(4.55)	
Immoral Traffic	7706	8323	8695	9363	9515	8796	6598	5510	5748	-25.4
Act	(6.66)	(6..86)	(6.61)	·(6.90)	(6073)	(6.12)	(4.61)	(3.92)	(3.72)	
Dowry	2647	2685	3578	3064	2876	3222	2816	2684	3592	35.7
Prohibition Act	(2.29)	(2.22)	(2.72)	(2.26)	(2.03)	(2.24)	(1.97)	(1.91)	(2.33)	
Other Acts	278	151	336	223	726	1166	2584	1089	1467	427.7
	(0.24)	(0.12)	(0.25)	(0.16)	(0.51)	(0.81)	(1.86)	(0.77)	(0.95)	
Total	115723	121264	131475	135771	141373	143795	143034	140601	154333	33.4
	(100)	(100)	(100)	(100)	(100)	(100)	(100)	(100)	(100)	

Source: GOI, Crime in India, 2001, National Crime Records Bureau, 2003 and 2005.

and psychological both in public and private life. This declaration was unprecedented, the first of its kind. It sets the standards and outlines the basic rights of women. Further delegates from 180 countries reached agreement on June 10, 2000 during the Beijing +5 conference at New York and called upon the governments for the prosecution of all forms of domestic violence including marital rape.

Domestic violence can be described as when one adult in a relationship misuses power to control another. It is the establishment of control and fear in a relationship through violence and other forms of abuse. The violence may involve physical abuse, sexual assault and threats. Some times it is more subtle, like making someone feel worthless, not letting them have any money, or not allowing them to leave the home. Social isolation and emotional abuse can have long-lasting effects as well as physical violence.

Domestic violence is not just hitting, or fighting, or an occasional argument. It is an abuse of power. The abuser tortures and controls the victim by calculated threats, intimidation, and physical violence. Although both men and women can be abused, in most cases, the victims are woman. Children in homes where there is domestic violence are also abused or neglected. Although the woman is usually the primary target, violence is sometimes directed towards children, and sometimes towards family members and friends. Many women in India are the victims of domestic violence.

Definition of Domestic Violence

The term 'domestic violence' is not exactly defined under the Indian laws. Under the Indian law the 'term' cruelty to wife' is being used to address this growing menace. The United Nations model legislation on 'domestic violence' defines domestic violence as:

All acts of gender -based physical, psychological abuse by family member against women in the family, ranging from simple assaults to aggravated physical battery, kidnapping, threats, intimidation, coercion, stalking, humiliating verbal abuse, forcible or unlawful entry, arson, destruction of property, sexual violence, marital rape, dowry or related violence, female genital mutilation, violence related to exploitation through prostitution, violence against household workers and attempts to commit such acts shall be termed "domestic violence".

The National Commission for Women defined domestic violence to connote:

"Domestic violence" means any of the following acts committed on a woman by her husband or any of his or her relatives, namely,

- any willful conduct which-
- is of such a nature as is likely to drive the woman out of the house or commit suicide or to injure herself ; or
- causes injury or danger to the life, limb or health (weather mental or physical) or the woman; or
- harassment which causes distress to a woman; or
- any act which compels the woman to have sexual intercourse against her will either with the husband or any of his relatives or with any other person : or
- any act which is unbecoming of the dignity of the woman: or
- any other act of omission or commission, which is likely to cause mental torture or mental agony to the woman.

Forms of Domestic Violence

Domestic Violence can take many forms and variations and can happen once in a while or all at the same time. Domestic violence can be Physical abuse, Sexual abuse, Emotional abuse, Economic abuse, and Psychological abuse.

Physical Abuse: Hitting, slapping, shoving, grabbing, pinching, biting, hair-pulling, etc. Physical abuse also includes denying a partner medical care or forceful use of alcohol and/or drug.

Sexual Abuse: Coercing or attempting to coerce any sexual contact or behavior without consent. Sexual abuse includes, but certainly not be limited to marital rape, attacks on private parts of the body, forcing sex after physical violence has occurred, or treating one in a sexual demeaning manner.

Emotional Abuse: Undermining an individual's sense of self-worth and/or self-esteem. This may include, but is not limited to constant criticism, diminishing one's abilities, name-calling, or damaging one's relationship with his or her children.

Economic Abuse: Economic abuse includes not sharing or using money as a family, prevention from going to work and withholding or taking money from wife or partner.

Psychological Abuse: Psychological abuse refers to public humiliation, constant criticism, verbal abuse, i.e. use of abusive language, instilling fear or threats and isolation or confinements.

Domestic violence can happen to anyone regardless of race, age, sexual orientation, religion, or gender. Domestic violence affects people of all socio-economic backgrounds and education levels. Domestic violence occurs in both heterosexual and same-sex relationships and can happen to intimate partners who are married, living together, or dating. Domestic violence not only affects those who are abused, but also has a substantial effect on family members, friends, co- workers, other witnesses, and the community at large. Children, who grow up witnessing domestic violence, are among those seriously affected by this crime. Frequent exposure to violence in the home not only predisposes children to numerous social and physical problems, but also teaches them that violence is a normal way of life - therefore, increasing their risk of becoming society's next generation of victims and abusers.

According to National Crime Records Bureau in India one crime against woman every three minutes, one rape every 29 minutes, one dowry death case every 77 minutes, one case of cruelty by husband and relatives every nine minutes.

The National Crime Records Bureau,(NCRB, Annual Report 2005), also recorded a total of 1,55,553 cases of violence against woman(VAW)including 18,359 cases of rape involving 18,376 victims, 34,175 cases of molestation, 15750 cases of kidnapping , 6,787 cases of dowry deaths and 58,319 cases of torture in 2005. Despite high rate of violence against woman, only 24 out of 28 states in India have established State Commission for Woman by 2005 a total of 1,172 cases of rape of the Scheduled Caste woman and a total of 640 cases of rape of the Scheduled Tribe women were recorded in 2005.

Ten thousands domestic violence cases by major states in India are reported against woman during 2006-2007 (After prevention of Domestic violence Act-2006) is presented in Table 3.

Table 3
State-Wise Domestic Violence Cases Against Women in India: 2006-07

State	*No. of cases*
Rajasthan	3440
Kerala	1028
Andhra Pradesh	331
Delhi	607
Maharashtra	603
Goa	603
Gujarat	315
Punjab	249
Haryana	235
Uttaranchal	145
Karnataka	124
Bihar	64
West Bengal	54
Orissa	12
Uttar Pradesh	00
Other states	1087

Source: According to Indira Jai Singh, Lawyers Collective (till July 2007).

Causes of Domestic Violence

There is no one single factor to account for violence perpetrated against women. Increasingly, research has focused on the inter-relatedness of various factors that help us to understand the problem within different cultural contexts.

Several complex and interconnected institutionalized social and cultural factors have kept women particularly vulnerable to the violence directed at them, all of them manifestations of historically unequal power relation between men and women. Factors contributing to these unequal power relations include: socio-economic forces, the family institution where power relations are enforced, fear of and control over female sexuality, belief in the inherent superiority of males, and legislation and cultural sanctions that have traditionally denied women and children an independent legal and social status.

Lack of economic resources underpins women's vulnerability to violence and their difficulty in extricating themselves from a violent relationship. The link between violence and lack of economic resources and dependence is circular. On the one hand, the threat and fear of violence keeps women from seeking employment, or, at best, compels them to accept low-paid, home-based exploitative labour. And on the other, without economic independence, women have no power to escape from an abusive relationship.

Cultural ideologies-both in industrialized and developing countries– provide 'legitimacy' for violence against women in certain circumstances. Religious and historical traditions in the past have sanctioned the chastising and beating of wives. The physical punishment of wives has been particularly sanctioned under the notion of entitlement and ownership of women. Male control of family wealth inevitably places decision-making authority in male hands, leading to male dominance and proprietary rights over women and girls.

The concept of ownership, in turn, legitimizes control over women's sexuality, which in many law codes has been deemed essential to ensure patrilineal inheritance. Women's sexuality is also tied to the concept of family honour in many societies. Traditional norms in these societies allow the killing of 'errant' daughters, sisters and wives suspected of defiling the honour of the family by including in forbidden sex, or marrying and divorcing without the consent of the family.

Excessive consumption of alcohol and other drugs has also been noted as a factor in provoking aggressive and violent male behaviour towards women and children. A survey of domestic violence in Moscow revealed that half the cases of physical abuse are associated with the husband's excessive alcohol consumption.

The isolation of women in their families and communities is known to contribute to increased violence, particularly if those women have little access to family or local organizations. On the other hand, women's participation in social networks has been noted as a critical factor in lessening their vulnerability to violence and in their ability to resolve domestic violence.

Lack of legal protection, particularly within the sanctity of the home, is a strong factor in perpetuating violence against women. Until recently, the public/private distinction that has ruled most legal systems has been a major obstacle to women's rights. Increasingly, however, States are seen as responsible for protecting the rights of women even in connection with offences committed within the home. Factors like Cultural, Economic, Legal and Political perpetuate domestic violence ate presented in Table 4.

Table 4
Factors That Perpetuate Domestic Violence

Cultural	• Gender- specific socialization
	• Cultural definitions of appropriate sex roles
	• Expectations of roles with in relationships
	• Belief in the inherent superiority of males
	• Values that give men proprietary rights over women and girls
	• Notion of the family as the private sphere and under male control
	• Customs of marriage (bride price/dowry)
	• Acceptability of violence as a means to resolve conflict.
Economic	• Women's economic dependence on men
	• Limited access to cash and credit
	• Discriminatory laws regarding inheritance, property rights, use of communal lands, and maintenance after divorce or widowhood.

Contd...

	• Limited access to employment in formal and informal sector
	• Limited access to education and training for men
Legal	• Lesser legal status of women either by written law and /or by practice
	• Laws regarding divorce, child custody, maintenance and inheritance
	• Legal definitions of rape and domestic abuse
	• Low levels of legal literacy among women
	• Insensitive treatment of women and girls by police and judiciary
Political	• Under- representation of women in power, politics, the media and in the legal and medical professions
	• Domestic violence not taken seriously
	• Nations of family being private and beyond control of the state
	• Risk of challenge to status quo/religious laws
	• Limited organisations of women as a political force
	• Limited participation of women in organized political system

Source: Heise, 1994.

Conclusions

Domestic violence on women is on the increase in India. Every day hundreds of women are physically, mentally, psychologically abused, tortured and also thrown out of the homes. Of all the forms of violence that women face, domestic violence remains the least reported and largely suppressed. Although the women are usually the primary target, violence is some times directed towards children, and some times towards family members and friends. Many women who suffer from domestic violence have little or no education. Economic insecurity, social stigma attached with separation is some of the important factors that force women to bear domestic violence. For the sake of their children women are prepared to tolerate anything. Moreover, women are also discouraged to come back to their parent's home as it would bring a bad name to the whole family. Though various women organisations are working very hard with well defined strategies, yet they have failed to address the issue of domestic violence specifically. It is in this background it is necessary for each one of us to understand the issue and the legal provisions for playing a reformist role to combat this growing violence.

References

Agnes, Flavia (1992), "Protecting Women Against Violence? Review of a Decade of Legislation on Violence against Women: 1980-1989", *Economic and Political Weekly,* 27 (17): WS 21-34.

Agnes, Flavia (1998), "Violence in the Family: Wife Beating". in Rehana Ghadially (ed.) Women in Indian Society-A Reader, Sage Publications, New Delhi.

Baxi, Mamta (2001), Violence for Equality: A Report on Nari Adalat, Gujarat, Tata Institute of Social Sciences, Mumbai.

Bhattacharya, R. (2004), Behind Closed Doors Domestic Violence in India, Sage Publications, New Delhi.

Ellisberg, M, Heise, L. and Shrader, E. (1999), Researching Violence against Women: A Practical Guide for Research and Advocates, Centre for Health and Gender Equity, Washington D.C.

Jai Singh, I. (1995), "Violence Against Women: The Indian Perspective" in J. Peters and A. Walpes (ed.) Women's Rights, Human Rights, Sage Publications, New Delhi.

Kelkar, Govind (1991), Violence Against Women in India: Perspective and Strategies, Asian Institute of Technology, Bangkok.

Mira Seta (2001), Women and Development: The Indian Experience, Crime Against Women", Sage Publications, New Delhi.

National Crime Record Bureau (2005), National Crime Record Bureau Report, New Delhi.

Poonacha, Veena and Divya Pandey (1999), Response to Domestic Violence in States of Karnataka and Gujarat, Research Centre for Women Studies, SNDT Women's University, Mumbai.

Prasad, Shally (1999), Medico-Legal Response to Violence against Women in India, Violence against Women, 5 (5) 478-506.

Singh, I. P. (1990), Indian Women: The Captured Beings, Intellectual Publication, New Delhi.

ELDER ABUSE: AN IMPEDIMENT FOR JUSTICE AND WELLBEING

*K. Suneetha**

Introduction

India has nearly 8 per cent of senior citizens in the population. This is expected to escalate to 11.8 per cent by 2015 and to 18.4 per cent by the year 2025 giving rise to a Silver boom. The society which was formerly protective is now breaking up. Elder abuse has never been considered a problem in India and has always been thought as a problem of western countries. In the changing scenario of 21st century of globalization, nuclear orientation and fragmentation with high ambition in younger generation, the issue of older abuse in India has reached a magnitude of hidden, underreported epidemic form. It raises many complexes, ethical, legal and clinical questions. Prevalence rates/estimates exist only in selected developed countries. Although estimates vary, it is generally believed that 4-6 per cent of the elderly are abused worldwide. (The word report on violence and health, 2002).

Elder abuse is defined as the physical, emotional or financial mistreatment and neglect of an elderly person by a family member [relative] or by a care giver (Decalmer and Glendenning, 1997). Elder abuse in domestic setting is a wide spread problem, possibly affecting hundreds of thousands of elderly people across the country. However, it is still largely hidden under the shroud of family secrecy; this type of abuse is grossly underreported. [National Center for Elder abuse]. Now-a-days, we have to suspect that an elderly person we know is being harmed physically or emotionally by a neglectful or overwhelmed caregiver or being preyed upon. Obviously many victims do not report their abuse due to shame,

* *Assistant Professor, Department of Social Work, Vikrama Simhapuri University, Nellore-524 001, (E-mail:suneethak2007@rediffmail.com)*

helplessness, dependence on the abuser, or inability to repent. Most often the abuser is an adult child, grandchild, spouse, or care giver of the victim. However abuse also occurs in institutions of care for the elderly by abusers unrelated to the victim. Abuse against older people is a matter of justice and communities must work together to prevent such abuses with multi-disciplinary approach involving all sections of the community (Chakrabarthi, 2004) to provide graceful ageing to the elderly. Here the Social workers place a crucial role.

Some of the studies which had been undertaken at international level were (Schraiber, et al. 2006, Lachs and colleagues, 1998, Goldstien, 1996) focused on elder abuse showed that elderly people are subjected to verbal, physical and financial abuse. In the United States between 1986 and 1996, the National centre on elder abuse recorded a 150 per cent increase in incidence of abuse reported by state adult protective services (UN 2002). Based on the best available estimates, between 1 and 2 million Americans 65 or older have been injured, exploited, or otherwise mistreated by someone on whom they depended for care or protection (Pavlik et al., 2001). The potential pool of adult children who can serve as caregivers is already decreasing, as a result of a variety of demographic trends, including divorce, smaller families, and increased workforce participation (Himes et al., 1996).

The elderly wellbeing is largely contingent on the economic capacity of the family unit (Vijaya Kumar, 2005) particularly in rural areas families suffer from economic crisis. Singh (1994-95) conducted a study with an aim of highlighting the indispensability of integration of the elderly with family for their proper care and protection in India. It was a rapid survey of 200 senior citizens from Lucknow city. The survey revealed that elder abuse is present in one or the other form. The results indicate that 24.5 per cent expressed lack of affection and belongingness in providing food, which they used to get earlier by family members and relatives, 39.5 per cent did not get medical care, 32 per cent did not get recreation and 64.5 per cent expressed that their presence was not considered essential by their family members. It is important to recognize that the aged can and do have an active role to play in the development of the family, the local Community and the nation at large.

Financial abuse is very common, especially with upper and middle class Indians. This kind of abuse involves illegal or improper use of elders' funds, property or assets. Gender differences emerged only in response to chronic financial strain (Krause and Keith, 1990). There is no retirement for women from domestic work. To supplement family income the aged women have to perform activities such as looking after the milching animals, household activities like cooking, sweeping, cleaning utensils, collection of firewood and making cow dung cakes for fuel purposes, working as seasonal labourer on low wages. These activities are beyond their physical stamina. A number of stressful life events increased when men and women become more involved in their social support networks. This is also true in the case of employed or working women as they are assigned hard/time bound tasks which are quite difficult during old age. Most of the women are facing this type of situation in their homes where they are voiceless, suffering calmly. (Suneetha, 2005 and Surekha Rao, 2010). Some elderly are institutionalized due to a space crunch at their own place. Insensitivity towards the needs of the elders; intentional or unintentional withholding of needed care is also present in so many families. Self neglect self-induced abuse is also observed in some elderly resulting in physical harm and mental anguish. This also leads the rising rates of the elderly wanting to die. (Mehta, 2000).

Physical, psychological, social abuse in the form of verbal abuse, exploitation, harassment, ill-treatment, deprivation and neglect is common among the elderly. Factors which might be causing elder abuse include decline of human and spiritual values, materialistic attitudes of the present society, emotional disturbances and individualistic attitudes of younger generation. Kapur (1997) opined that through the inculcation of human and spiritual values through self-realization, the abuse of the elderly can be minimized and also suggested that the younger and older people must accept to get counselling in solving their problems at an early stage with the help of professional counsellors. The government is providing social security programmes for the elderly such as old age pension scheme, old age homes, day care centres, health services, life insurance, Annapurna schemes, travel concessions, etc. The social worker has to facilitate the elderly to utilize these needs. National Policy of older persons visualizes that the state will extend support in the areas of: Financial security, Health Care, Shelter, Welfare, Protection against abuse and exploitation and Opportunities for development of older person's potential. But Preventive and remedial interventions have been unsystematic, episodic, and poorly evaluated till now. To achieve the desired goals (National Policy of older persons) Ministry of Social Justice and Empowerment should take necessary steps to prepare action plan and implementation of programmes of the elderly especially to reduce elder abuse which is growing alarmingly and underreported. Elder abuse is a case of human rights violation. (Katyayani, 2008). According to Barada(2010) the rights of the aged are *to be treated as a person, be treated as an adult, enjoy fair chances on own merits, right to be romantic, right to be interested in public life and right to professional help if necessary;* which are violated in to-to by the family members, caregivers and by the community at large.

Methodology

In this context a study has been carried out in Tirupati rural with few objectives such as:

- to understand socio-economic and demographic status of the respondents,
- to assess their health status and life satisfaction
- to know the elderly perceptions regarding the elder abuse and
- To study the prevalence of elder abuse in study area.

The researcher conducted this study with descriptive and explorative design to find out the facts with regard to prevalence of elder abuse in study area. By using purposive sampling technique a sample 400 elderly were selected from eight villages of Tirupati rural Mandal. These 8 villages were randomly chosen from a total of 42 villages in Tirupati rural. Structured interview schedule, focus group discussions were used to elicit information from the respondents regarding objectives. The collected data was analyzed and inferences were drawn based on the results.

Findings of the Study

A little above half (52%) are in the age group of 60-65 years, most of the elderly (64%) are able to read and write and had primary education. Nearly three fourths are currently married, and three fifths of the elderly are staying with spouse and their son. Most of the elderly (56%) were having 2-3 children. Close to three fifths (59%) of elderly are living in their own house. The monthly household income of the elderly is Rs3000-6000. The study results revealed that most of the elderly (58%) are not having income of their own. Two-fifths of the elderly are financially dependent on others. One fifth of the elderly are engaged in economic activity and most of them are having assets on their name (52%).Two fifths of the respondents main source of income is old age pension which is very meagre.

The elderly faced various types of abuse such as showing disrespect being the most common form of abuse followed by verbal abuse, neglect, economic abuse and emotional abuse. 44% of the elderly are of the view that negligence is elder abuse; they felt that they are neglected most of the time (54%). More than two fifths stated that the family members are busy with their own work/life and neglected them. One fifth of respondents faced abuse due to property issues. The elderly feel that elderly abuse constitutes emotional abuse (40%), verbal abuse (50%), economic abuse (47%), showing disrespect (57%) and physical abuse (63%). Negligence (44%) property issues (35%) fear of institutionalization (56%). (Figure 2) Srinivas and Vijailakshmi(2001) study also support the results as the 81 per cent sample in their study faced problem of verbal abuse, Physical abuse than their male counterparts. More than half of the elderly (56%) are unwilling to take any action when they faced abuse nor registered any case. Unwillingness to take any action against abuse stems from the perception among the elderly that 'sense of shame'(34%) in the community, fear of further abuse(38%), love(15%) and concern(13%) towards family members. (Figure 1)

The outcome of focus group reveals that , the participants of all the focus groups initially talked about emotional problems such as 'lack of emotional support', 'neglect by the family members', 'feeling of insecurity', 'loss of dignity', 'maltreatment', 'disrespect' by the family. However, not a single person was willing to label it as "abuse". They linked abuse to very severe acts of violence, which they all seemed to agree was abnormal and did not happen in our societies. Further the results revealed that awareness about laws; policies and programmes against elderly abuse is low among the respondents. Elderly awareness about Laws (25%), policies (17%), programmes (34%), Lack of awareness about the agencies which are providing services (26%) (Figure 4). Help Age India study on 'report on elder abuse in India',2010 reveal that elderly awareness is higher in Delhi with 53.8%, lowest in Bhopal with 8%.

The study clearly indicates that the elderly are not satisfied with their present living status. Two fifths of the elderly (40%) feel neglected sometimes while 34% feel always neglected (Figure 3). Similar observations made by Rajadurai (2010) in Chennai that 54% of the elderly are not living with children and 71.4% feel that their families don't respect them. More than two-fifths (47%) of the elderly reported that the family members are busy with their own work/lives and thus neglect them. Elderly stated that abuser is more from the family members such as son and daughter-in-law emerging as the major abusers. Nearly 50% of the elderly reported abuse due to non-fulfillment of basic necessities. More than half of the elderly (56%) didn't take any action when they faced abuse. Most of the elderly (94%) didn't complain against the abuser and those who registered complaint hasn't taken any concrete steps towards it. Where the provisions under The Maintenance and Welfare of Parents and Senior Citizens Act, 2007 are also not utilized by them. Shuba (2006) in her study at Delhi state identified that elder abuse is grossly underreported in India as they are not willing to discuss it. But some studies elicited information on elder abuse with help of Focus group discussions.

Table 1
Respondents Perception about Neglect

Neglect to	*Per cent*
Assist in personal hygiene	54%
Provide food,	78%
Provide medical care	65%
Provide physical and psychological support	56%
provide clothing , shelter	74%
Talk or conversation	65%

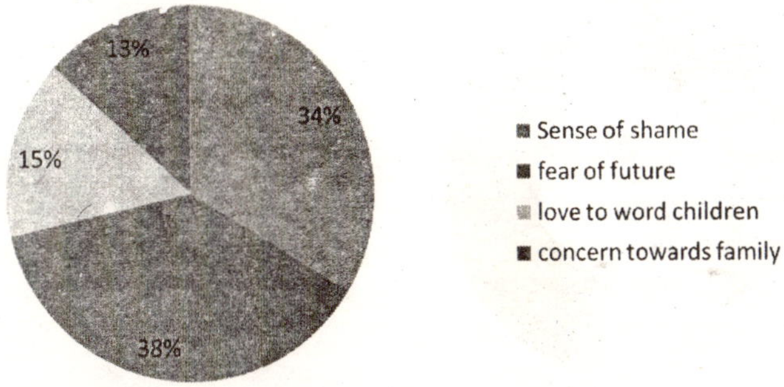

Figure 1: Causes for Unwillingness to Take Action Against Abuser

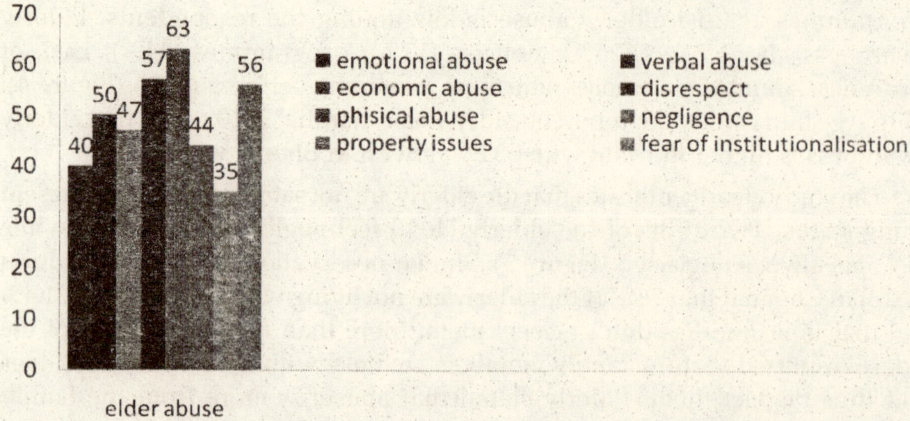

Figure 2: Types of Abuse Experienced by the Elderly

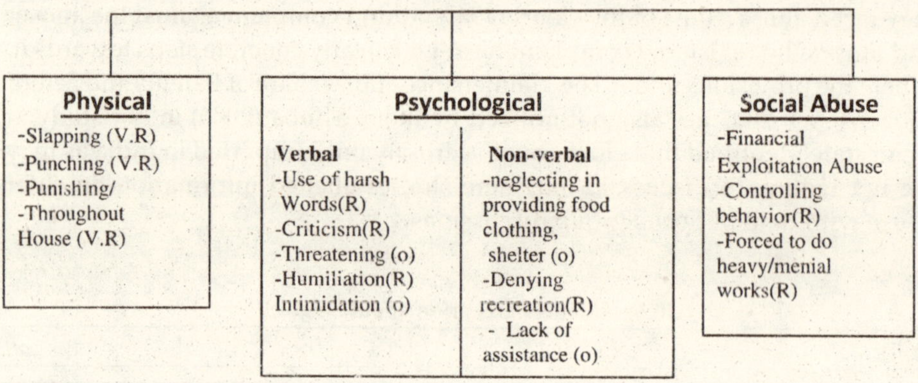

R= Regular, O = Occasional, V.R= Very Rare.

Figure 3: Frequency of Abuses Experienced by the Respondents

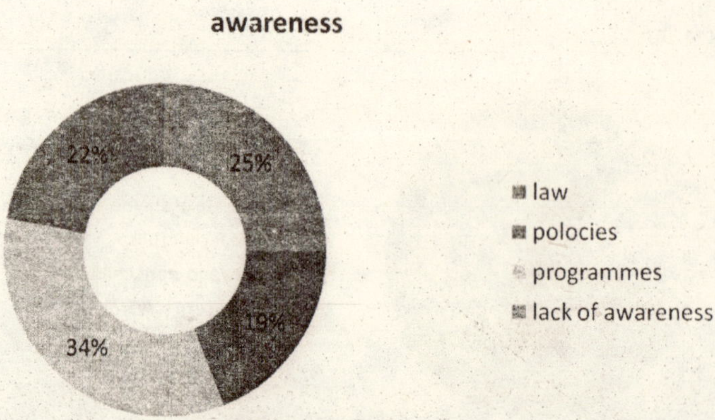

Figure 4: Respondents Awareness About Laws, Policies and Programmes

Conclusion

The population of the aged is increasing all over the world. Older people are vulnerable not only to the infirmities and suffering associated with disease and disability, but also to neglect, victimization, and exploitation by others, including their caregivers. In this respect, protecting older people from abuse is an important element of the broad challenge of ensuring quality of life of the elders. The potential pool of adult children who can serve as caregivers is already decreasing, as a result of a variety of demographic trends, including smaller families, and increased workforce participation ,individualistic attitudes etc. These factors increase elder abuse as well as pressure on families caring for their elderly relatives and also are likely to increase the demand for institutional care. This study results clearly visualize that the elderly rights are grossly violated by their respective family members. Upholding the rights of the aged Help Age India, Silver line, CARE international etc are advocates for the older persons rights, who constitutes 90 million (present estimate) to help them live with dignity.

Need of Intervention

The complexity of interrelationships factors of elder abuse such as physical and psychological status, economic resources and other social factors call for the need of intervention by professional social workers. Educating aged, family members on how to cope with the associated problems of the ageing, educating elderly on how to adjust with various situations come across in the family for graceful ageing, educating on stress management, counselling for the victims and abusers, sensitizing the community about elder abuse and recognizing early mistreatment through constituting community action teams to reduce elder abuse. The social worker by using the methods like case work, group work, community organization and social work research and with the skills and techniques of social work can intervene to reduce elder abuse and improve their status.

The main goals of social work intervention with elderly are three fold:

(i) Ameliorative - when problems already cropped up i.e. when the elderly facing abuse, through individual and group counselling (family) will be facilitated to reduce elder abuse.

(ii) Preventive - for the anticipated problems like weak/disturbed family dynamics, lack of proper adjustment; family counselling will be provided to strengthen family ties for good adjustment between the family members.

(iii) Promotional or developmental - help the elderly to enhance their social functions, like in utilization of human resource effectively, to develop their income generating capacity and be a resource to community towards promoting national growth and development as well as to enhance their wellbeing.

Recommendations

- Establishing more counselling centres to reduce elder abuse by strengthening family dynamics/system through counselling for both victims and caregivers.
- In-depth research is needed as elderly abuse hidden/under reported issue. So it is essential to identify the abused, and arrive at the exact cause of the abuse.
- To provide more knowledge on policies, legislations which are existing there by making the elderly to avail above said.
- More awareness is to be created through print and electronic media about care and welfare services that are provided for the elderly.
- '*Community action teams*' are to be setup to identify incidence of elderly abuse and nip them in bud stage as for as possible to reduce elder abuse and promote their well being.

References

Baradha (2010), "Healthy Ageing: Central Component of Development Agenda", *Social Welfare,* Vol. 57, No. 7, pp. 12-13.

Decalmer and Glendenning, F. (1997), "The Mistreatment of Elderly People", New Delhi, Sage Publications.

Glodstein, M. (1996), "Elder Mistreatment and PTST" In *Ageing and Post Traumatic Stress Disorder,* P. E. Ruskin & J. A. Talbots, Eds. Washington DC: American Psychiatric Association.

Jamuna, D. (2003), "Issues of Elderly Care and Elder Abuse in Indian Context", *Journal of Ageing and Social Policy,* Vol. 15, Issue 2 and 3.

Lachs, M. S. (1998), "The Mortality of Elder Mistreatment", *Journal of American Medical Association,* Vol. 280, pp. 428-432.

Pavlik, V.N., D. J. Hyman, N.A. Festa, and C. Bitondo Dyer (2001), Quantifying the Problem of Abuse and Neglect in Adults—Analysis of a Statewide Database. *Journal of the American Geriatrics Society* Vol. 49, No. 1, pp. 45-48.

Schraiber, Liliablima, Anaflavia PLD Oliveira, Marcia Therezacouto (2006), "Violence and Health: Recent Scientific Studies", *Revsaude* Publication, 40.

Shuba Soneja (2006), "Elderly Abuse in India", *Country Report for World Health Organization,* Help Age India.

Srinivas S. and Vijai Lakshmi, B. (2001), "Abuse and Neglect of the Elderly in Families", *Indian Journal of Social Work,* Special Issue on Family Voilence,Vol. 62, No. 3, pp. 272-275.

The World Report on Violence and Health (2002), "Elder Abuse: The South Asian Context", Published by *The International Longevity Centre* (India), Pune, 2006.

United Nations (2002), "United Nations Department of Public Information. DPI/2264 March, 2002. United Nations Report on Ageing. UN Department of Economics and Social Affairs.

WHO (1995), "A Global Response to Elder Abuse and Neglect: Building Primary Health Care Capacity to Deal with the Problem World", Geneva, WHO, 2006.

VIOLENCE AGAINST WOMEN IN INDIA: ISSUES AND POLICIES

*N. Radhakrishnan**

Introduction

The horizon of life is painfully limited by the narrow concept of women's position in the human society. Violence against women is criminally luxurious. Women in the Indian society have been the hapless victims of humiliation, torture and exploitation for centuries and centuries. But today, they are being gradually recognized as vital catalysts in accelerating the material, moral and spiritual prosperity of their men folk. Ideologies, institutional practices and the army of sensual delights have contributed much to their harassment over the years. Some of these behavioural practices thrive even today. In spite of the legislative measures adopted to better the societal status of women after Independence, the spread of education and women's gradual economic independence, countless women still continue to be the victims of phosphorescent violence. They are beaten, kidnapped, raped, burnt and murdered. The lamps of equality and justice that have been kindled have been put out by the storms of masculine anarchy.

"The status of women indicates the character of the country" vouchsafed Pandit Jawaharlal Nehru. The social standing of any society is determined by the social status of its women. Women have played a pivotal role in the evolution of man and his progeny. They continue to be the edifices of tolerance, personifications of sacrifice, effulgent emblems of selflessness and towers of grace.

The society should develop and flower into a just and balanced system for both men and women. As Mahatma

---

* *Reader in Economics, Muthurangam Govt. Arts College, Vellore–632 002, Tamil Nadu, India.*

Gandhi believed, intellectually, mentally and spiritually woman should run a race with man and should not continue to be caught up in the ever-tightening noose of exploitation. In absence of woman's fundamental rights, the society will be dull and drab like the sky without its stars. But everywhere in the world women are accorded a lower status than men. Describing the status of women all over the world, Gustave Speth in his foreword to Human Development Report, 1995 writes, "Women still constitute 70 per cent of the world's poor, and 2/3rd of the world's illiterate. They occupy 14 per cent of managerial and administrative jobs, 10 per cent of parliamentary seats and 6 per cent of Cabinet positions. In many legal systems they are still unequal".

In recent years, there has been an alarming increase in atrocities and violence against women in the country. It is estimated that the growth rate of crime against women would be higher than the population growth rate by 2011, which implies that progressively a greater number of women are becoming victims of violence. The United Nations Commission on the status of women defines violence against women to include "any act of gender-based violence that results in, or is likely to result in, physical, sexual or psychological harm or suffering to women". Throughout human history, women in several Continents have been considered as a physically weaker sex. The gender differences and bias existing globally place women in various disadvantageous positions. High standards and values of life are debased like the colour and texture of the contemporary society. The crumbling mansion of woman's life is made to stand on the weakening pillars of injustice, inequality and indifference. Crimes against women are assertion of dominance over them. As a matter of fact, the problem of violence on women is not something new or sensational. The low social, economic and political profile of women coupled with the other miseries get their life crushed and ruined. Moreover, Violence against women is not considered as violence at all because of the general acceptance of man's superiority over them. Women themselves also do not consider it as violence because of their misconstrued religious values and the fears of misinterpreting it as a social and spiritual question. And thus, it is at times, a self-wrought torture. It is extremely lamentable but women welcome it as a necessary evil. In daily life they are generally defined and abused by sex and it is said that even if all men are not potential molesters, rapists, batterers or torturers, majority of women could be considered as potential victims of violence and crime and flickering flames of self-defacement.

Violence Against Women: Situation in India

The incidents of total crime in the country are on the increase year by year, but the rate of increase in crime against women is higher than the rate of increase in other crimes. The following table depicts a picture of crimes against women in the country from 1992 to 2001.

Table 1
Total Number of Crimes Against Women in India

Year	*Total no. of Crimes*	*Crimes Against Women*	*Women Crime in Percentage of Total Crimes*
1992	16,89,341	79,031	4.68
1993	16,29,936	83,954	5.15
1994	16,35,251	91,012	5.56
1995	16,95,696	97,459	5.74
1996	17,09,576	1,05,274	6.15
1997	17,19,820	1,10,184	6.40
1998	17,78,815	1,19,012	6.69
1999	17,64,629	1,23,122	6.97
2000	17,71,084	1,28,320	7.24
2001	17,69,308	1,30,725	7.38
	r (Growth Rate) = 0.20		*2.18*

Source: Crime in India Reports for the respective years.

It may be observed that while the total crimes reported under Indian Penal Code had registered a growth rate of 0.20 per cent per annum during 1992 to 2001, the growth rate of crime against women had been 2.18 per cent per annum. As a result, crime against women under IPC, which constituted 4.68 per cent of total crimes in 1992, reveals a continuous increase during the last decade and it constitutes 7.38 per cent of total crimes in 2001.

The list of crimes that are committed against women extend from simple harassment to even denying them the very right to exist. Man is a degenerate angel who derives pleasure out of torturing women within the four walls, in lonely places and even in public places in front of others. As per Crime in India Report 2001, four molestation cases, one sexual harassment case, six cases of cruelty by husband and relatives, two rape cases and one dowry death cases are reported every hour in the country.

The table reveals that among the different types of crime committed against women, torture (both physical and mental) constitutes the most important form of crime followed by molestation and rape. The incidence of all types of crimes had increased in the years mentioned above except sexual harassment, which had decreased marginally, during the period by 9.7 per cent. Highest per centage variation was observed in case of torture followed by molestation. This derives into lime light that the gates of paradise of bliss for women are under the shadows of man's ghastly deeds of crime and cruelty.

Table 2
Incidence of Different Crimes Against Women in India

Crime Head	*Year* 1994	1995	1996	1997	1998	1999	2000	2001	2002	2003	2004	2005	2006	2007	2008	2009	% *Variation in 2009 over 2008*
Rape	12351	13754	14846	15330	15151	15468	16496	16075	NA	15847	18233	18359	19348	20737	21467	21397	-0.3
Kidnapping and Abduction	12998	14063	14877	15617	16351	15962	15023	14645	NA	13296	15578	15750	17414	20416	22939	25741	12.2
Dowry Death	4935	5092	5513	6006	6975	6699	6995	6851	NA	6208	7026	6787	7618	8093	8172	8383	2.6
Torture	25946	31127	35246	36592	41376	43823	45778	49170	NA	50703	58121	58319	63128	75930	75930	89546	10.1
Molestation	24117	28475	28939	30764	30959	32311	32940	34124	NA	32939	34567	34175	36617	38734	40413	38711	-4.2
Sexual Harassment	10496	4756	5671	5796	8054	8858	11024	9746	NA	12325	10001	9984	9966	10950	12214	11009	-9.9
Importation of Girls	167	191	182	78	146	1	64	114	NA	46	89	149	67	61	67	48	-28.3
Sati Prevention Act	2	27	0	1	0	0	0	0	NA	0	0	1	0	0	1	0	-100
Immoral Traffic (P) Act	7547	8447	7706	8323	8695	9363	9515	8796	NA	5510	5748	5908	4541	3568	2659	2474	-6.9
Indecent Representation of Women (P) Act	389	539	96	73	190	222	662	1052	NA	1043	1378	2917	1562	1200	1025	845	-17.6
Dowry Prohibition Act			2647	2685	3578	3064	2876	3222	NA	2684	3592	3204	4504	5623	5555	5650	1.7
Total	98948	106471	115723	121265	131475	135771	141373	143795	NA	140601	154333	155553	164765	185312	195856	203804	4.1

Source: National Crime Records Bureau, New Delhi.

The distribution of different crimes against women reported in the year 2009 is shown in the Figure below.

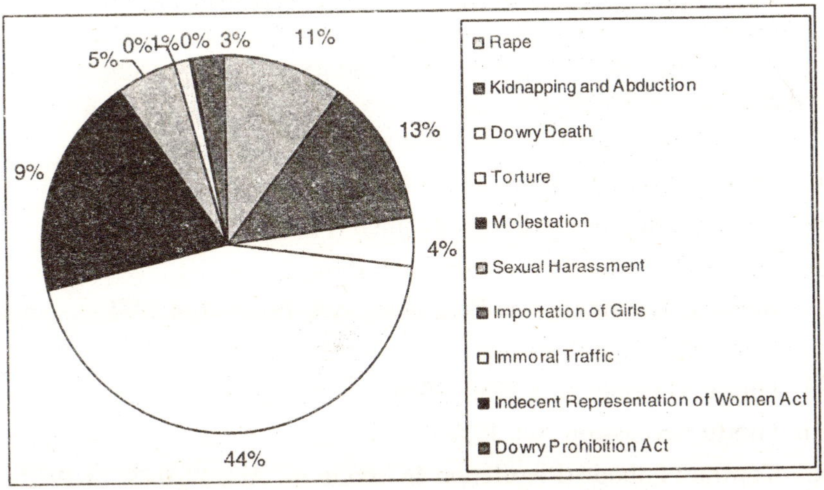

The Pie chart shows that torture constitutes the largest proportion of total crimes under IPC, followed by molestation, kidnapping, abduction and rape. Importation of girls, Sati Prevention and indecent representation of women constitute a very insignificant proportion (0.08 per cent) of total crimes against women in 2009 and therefore does not find place in the chart. Women should be lifted out of the slough of shame and tyranny of man. Unless stringent action is taken, mere endorsement of Acts will neither elevate the spirit nor illumine the intellect of man.

Legislative Measures–Legal Rights of Women

Women are also the victims of forced violence or crime commonly recognized as 'murder', 'robbery', 'cheating' and soon. The crimes, which are directed specifically against women, are characterized as 'Crimes Against Women':

The Crimes Identified Under the Indian Penal Code (IPC)

(i) Rape (Section 376 IPC)

(ii) Kidnapping & Abduction for different purposes (Section 363 - 373 IPC)

(iii) Homicide for Dowry, Dowry Deaths or their attempts (Section 302/304-B of IPC).

(iv) Torture, both mental and physical (Section 498- A of IPC).

(v) Molestation (Section 354 of IPC).

(vi) Sexual harassment (Section 509 of IPC) (referred to in the past as Eve-teasing)

(vii) Importation of girls (upto 21 years of age) (Section 366-B of IPC).

The Crimes Identified Under the Special Laws

Admittedly not all laws are gender specific but the provisions of various laws which affect women significantly have been reviewed Periodically by the Government and amendments have been carried out to keep pace with the emerging requirements. Some Acts which have special provisions to safeguard women and their interests are:

i. Commission of Sati (Prevention) Act, 1987 (3 of 1988).
ii. Dowry Prohibition Act, 1961 (28 of 1961).
iii. Indecent Representation of Women (Prohibition) Act, 1986.
iv. Immoral Traffic (Prevention) Act, 1956.
v. Medical Termination of Pregnancy Act, 1971 (34 of 1971).
vi. Child Marriage Restraint Act, 1929 (19 of 1929).
vii. Hindu Marriage Act, 1955 (25 of 1955).
viii. Hindu Succession Act, 1956 (3 of 1956).
ix. Contract Labour (Regulation & Abolition) Act, 1970 (37 of 1970).
x. Equal Remuneration Act, 1976 (25 of 1976).
xi. Factories Act, 1948 (63 of 1948) as amended in 1976.
xii. Maternity Benefit Act, 1961, (53 of 1961).
xiii. Criminal Law (Amendment) Act, 1983.
xiv. Special Marriage Act, 1954.
xv. The Family Courts Act, 1954.
xvi. Employees State Insurance Act, 1948.
xvii. Plantation Labour Act, 1951.

Steps Taken to Curb Violence Against Women

Under the Constitution of India law and order is a state subject. The responsibility for dealing with enforcement of he concerned Acts, therefore, rests with the state Governments. The registration of cases, investigation, detection and prevention of the crimes against women are primarily with State Government/Union Territory Administrations. However, the Government of India has initiated a number of healthy amendments apart from legislative changes in the relevant Acts. Instructions/guidelines have been issued to the State Governments/Union Territory administrations to effectively enforce legislation relating to crimes against women and monitor the enforcement.

The Minister of Human Resource Development had written, during August 2000 to all State Home Ministers stressing the need for including gender sensitization modules, a component of training courses, for enforcement of machinery in the State level Police Training Academies and also on the need for gender sensitization of judiciary. NGOs have been constituted to monitor the implementation of the Supreme Court's guidelines.

Various statutes exist which recognize women's specific crimes both social and physical, and the need to combat them. This has led to various proactive and preventive measures including protective legislation for women. The impact of these measures and legislation, however, requires to be strengthened. The Government has also been strengthening the existing legislations and developing new institutional machineries from time to time through extensive research and review. In addition to gender sensitization of law enforcement personnel it has set up helpful means like short stay homes, hostels for working women and rehabilitation centre for victims of violence. The Central Social Welfare Board is maintaining Family Counselling Centres (FCCs) to provide rehabilitative service to women and children who are victims of atrocities and family mal-adjustment. At present, 17 FCCs are functioning in the Capital Cities of Kerala, West Bengal, Orissa, Tripura, Pondicherry, Assam, Karnataka, Manipur, Goa, Maharashtra, Punjab, Haryana, Meghalaya, Nagaland, Uttar Pradesh, Sikkim, Tarnjl Nadu and Madhya Pradesh.

In order to address the phenomenon of domestic violence, which is widely prevalent in remaining largely invisible, the Government had introduced a Legislation entitled 'Protection from Domestic Violence Bill, 2002' in the Lok Sabha on 8th March, 2002, to empower the Magistrates to provide protection and necessary relief to victims of domestic violence. The Bill envisages that the protection officers would assist victims of domestic violence in getting access to shelter homes, health care, legal advice and so on and so forth.

'Crimes Against Women's Cells' have been set up in the states of Andhra Pradesh, Punjab, Orissa, Rajasthan, Tamil Nadu, Uttar Pradesh, Himachal Pradesh, Karnataka, Madhya Pradesh and in the Union Territories of Chandigarh, Delhi and Pondicherry.

During the Women's Empowerment Year, 2001, the Human Resource Department had written to all State Governments to set up District level committees headed by the District Magistrates to review and monitor cases of crimes against women, State Governments such as Andhra Pradesh, Chhatisgarh, Haryana, Kerala, Madhya Pradesh, Meghalaya, Mizorarm, Orissa, Punjab and Uttar Pradesh have set up such Committees.

The Government of India has also initiated steps to organize an effective campaign to sensitize the public about violence against women and also initiated action to compile and collate statistical information pertaining to seven types of crimes against women. These are (i) rape (Section 376 of Indian Penal Code), (ii) causing miscarriage (Section 312 to 316), (iii) harassment, both mental and physical in a marital relationship and offences relating to marriage (Chapter XX of IPC), (iv) dowry death (Section 304 B), (v) molestation as defined by Section 354 of Indian Penal Code, (vi) kidnapping and abduction (Section 366), and (vii) procuration of minor girls (Section 366 A).

Conclusion

In recent years, there has been a global campaign for elimination of violence against women, which indicates the seriousness of the problem of atrocities committed against women throughout the world. The need for protection of rights of women had gained global recognition during the International Decade of Women (1975-85) and has steadily gained momentum since then. This recognition became an International Law in 1979 when the U.N. General Assembly adopted the Convention on the Elimination of all Forms of Discrimination Against Women (CEDAW). India in 1993 joined other countries of the world and ratified CEDAW and committed itself to work for elimination of all types of discriminations which would place women at a disadvantage.

In the context of increase in different forms of crime against women, an analysation of the causes, consequences and concern at the family, society and the Government level assumes importance for eradication of such crimes. With scientific and technological advancement and urbanization, changes are witnessed in the personal life style and living standard of the people. Social ethos are shifting from bad to worse and all these factors are supposed to be contributing towards increase in crime against women in India.

An effective analysation of the crimes in relation to education, income, social attitudes and urbanisation will help in arriving at some strategic interventions needed at different levels for ensuring a social set up that will allow women to live with dignity and not as second rate citizens or marketable commodities.

The Constitution of India bestows on every citizen equality of status and equal opportunities. No discrimination should be made on grounds of sex, religion, or caste. All the citizens, have the same right to an adequate means of livelihood. But in practice, discrimination against women take roots from their very birth or even sometimes before birth. The gender inequity endemic in education, health, economic and political spheres relegates women to the status of second rate citizens and atrocities against women is a manifestation of the subordinate social status of women and girls.

It is true that all types of crime are on the increase in the country along with increase in population and progress of the economy. But the rate of growth of crime against women is much faster than that of total crime. The list of crimes that are committed against women seems to be endless extending from simple harassment to even denying them the very right to exist. The rate of crime against women per one lakh women population is officially estimated to be around 26, but in practice it would be much higher than this because quite a good number of crimes against women are never reported and brought to the daylight.

It is difficult for a single woman to raise her voice against injustice that is done to her whether within the family or outside. It is essential that more and more of women's Organisations are to be developed to take up the issues of women and to create an awareness among them. These Organisations can stage public meetings and discussions with general public to create an environment of hostility against specific offenders. Through demonstrations and poster campaigns on women's oppression, women can bring into lime light all sorts of atrocities against them, especially oppression of female workers in organised as well as unorganised sector. False ethical values and gender differences are to be replaced by high moral patterns, and effective civil code. Women-victims are to be lifted from the depths of degradation to the greatest heights of glory. The Government and Women's Welfare Associations should apply the key of justice to open the lock of equality. No woman is wax in the hands of her man. No woman should be broken down by endless torture. Her helplessness, frustration and despair should not get her life-springs dry up.

References

Bedabati Mohanty (2005), Violence Against Women, Kanishka Publishers, Distributors New Delhi.

Bela Rani Sharma (1999), Women Marriage, Family Violence & Divorce, Mangal Deep Publishers, Jaipur.

Rajkumar (2000), Violence Against Women, Anmol Publishers Pvt. Ltd. New Delhi.

Ram Ahuja (2004), Social Problems in India, Rawat Publications, New Delhi.

Sudhir, H. Jubita Hajarimayum (2005), Violence Against Women, Akansha Publishing House, New Delhi.

National Crime Record Bureau, India.

CHILD SEXUAL ABUSE: SNATCHING THE SMILE FOREVER

*Deepanshi** *& Anjali**

> *Child abuse is a problem no one really talks about. Abuse and neglect is the number one cause of injury to children in the country. More children die of abuse or neglect than of natural causes.*
>
> – DONNA MILLER

As per the World Health Organisation, 'Child sexual abuse is the involvement of a child in sexual activity that he or she does not fully comprehend, is unable to give informed consent to, or for which the child is not developmentally prepared and cannot give consent, or that violate the laws or social taboos of society. Child sexual abuse is evidenced by this activity between a child and an adult or another child who by age or development is in a relationship of responsibility, trust or power, the activity being intended to gratify or satisfy the needs of the other person.'[1] This could include sexual kissing, touching, and oral, anal, or vaginal sex. Not all sexual abuse involves body contact, though. Showing of private parts ("flashing"), forcing children to watch pornography, verbal pressure for sex, and exploiting children as prostitutes or for pornography can be sexual abuse as well[2].

The instances of child sexual abuse in India are very common but most of them do not come into light because of the conservative views of the people and the community does not talk about sex at all. There is a conspiracy of silence around the subject and a very large percentage of people feel that this is a largely western problem and that child sexual abuse does not happen in India.[3] According to a government commissioned survey, almost 53% of the children in the country get sexually abused but do not report the incident to anyone.[4]

---

* *2nd year students of Dr. Ram Manohar Lohiya National Law University, Lucknow (UP).*

This article explores the law in different countries on this issue of child abuse and the current legislation, conventions that are in force. In doing so, the article talks about psychological effects on a child, when s/he suffers with sexual abuse and the provisions provided under UN Convention, European Union and Indian laws dealing with matters of sexually abused children. It then focuses on the role of media, which should more be of a protector rather than spoiler; media must take care of child's right to privacy. This article concludes there has been no proper remedy for a sexually abused child and the words of the proposed Bill should be converted into implementation.

Compartive Study of Child Sexual Abuse with Other Countries

Sexual abuse has no acceptable level of expression like other abuses. UN convention on rights of the child considers 'best interest of the child' as this concept has become an international legal concept. There are provisions regarding Child Abuse in other countries which give protection to children and punish the perpetrators. The States in Australia generally have jurisdiction over justice and criminal law prosecution, and all offences against children are tried by the law of the State in which they were committed. [5]In the United States, child abuse prosecutions usually fall within the State jurisdictions so there is a variation in the law across states. However the government has taken initiatives to bring about uniformity in child protection laws by providing funds to the States if they enact federal statutes on the same.[6] The Adam Walsh Child Protection and Safety act of 2006 protects the people, children in particular from violent sexual offenders by providing for registration before an offender is released from the prison and also authorises the involuntary and indefinite confinement of persons who are suspicious of being sexually dangerous.[7] The Children Act of 1989 is the legislation in England which provides for protection of children from family abuse.[8]

Legal Provisions for Child Sexual Abuse

In early times rights of a child were not given very much importance. But in present era of globalisation we have different kinds of legislations, conventions and recommendations for the child sexual abuse protection of a child.

- *UN Convention on Rights of a Child:* This convention provides for protection of children against abuses as under–

  Article 19(1) of the UN Convention says that parties should take steps to protect the child from all types of violence when he is under the care of his parents or guardians.[9]

- *European Convection of Human Rights (ECHR):* Article 3 acknowledges the right to freedom from inhuman and degrading treatment.[10] This provision has been explicitly associated with cases of child abuse and neglect.[11]

- *Indian Position:* In India there is no particular law on sexual abuse of a child, they are treated under adult laws only. There is no clear cut definition of sexual abuse.

  Indian Penal Code (IPC): Under section 372-373 punishes the offender for buying and selling of minor girls for prostitution. Section 375 provides punishment for rape and section 377 punishes unnatural offenses.[12]

  Suppression of Immoral Traffic in Women and Girls Act, 1956: Section 5 to 10 punishes prostitution, inducing, taking woman or girl for prostitution.

  These are certain provisions where child sexual abuse is treated in India.

Role of Media: Child's Right to Privacy

Media is not supposed to report and disclose the identity of a person without his consent, who have being sexually assaulted. It is against the provisions of law which says–

> *"No report in any newspaper, magazine, news-sheet or visual media of any inquiry regarding a juvenile in conflict with law or a child in need of care and protection under this Act shall disclose the name, address or school or any other particulars calculated to lead to the identification of the juvenile or child nor shall any picture of any such juvenile or child be published".*[13]

Any publication of identity of abused child is only permitted when some inquiring authority is working in the interest of child. Similarly under section 228A of Indian penal code disclosure of identity of victim is punishable. As in Aarushi-Hemraj murder case, media has publicised the matter so much that it even affects opinion and judiciary verdict. There shall be some restrictions put on media in this regard.

Even 172nd Report of the Law Commission (2000), dealing with the review of rape laws suggested that the testimony of a minor in the case of child sexual abuse should be recorded at the earliest possible opportunity in the presence of a Judge and a child support person.[14] So media must be cautious while revealing identity of a person.

Psychological Effect on Child

Together with physical impact like penetration may amounts to genital damage or sexually transmitted disease, sexual abuse of child may also have psychological repercussions and later on difficulties in building up adult relationships. Sexual abuse is more likely to cause long term psychological, life altering damage than any other form of abuse.

Traumatic dynamics of sexual abuse are–

- An impact of the child's sexual development.
- The experience of betrayal by a trusted individual.

- Powerlessness, which may be reinforced by threats of violence or coercion
- Stigmatisation leading to feelings of shame and an assumption of responsibility for the abuse by the victim.[15]

Efforts to Protect Sexually Abused Children: Suggessions

In India as mentioned above, there is no clear cut law on this matter, although Bill is pending in Parliament which requires some concrete legal provisions and definitions of child sexual abuse. Other steps could be:

Proposed Bill on the Protection of Children from Sexual Assault, 2010

Bill aims to protect rights of children to privacy and confidentiality. It also provides for special courts for trial and rigorous punishment. But unfortunately this bill is in the stage of inter-ministerial consultation. Due to rapid increase in rate of crimes there is an urgent need of legislation to be passed by parliament which clearly describes child sexual abuse.

Educating Children About Such Issues

We must try educating children with such issues enlighten them by helping them distinguish between 'good' and 'bad' touch, or providing sex education in schools can also be productive.

Behaviour of the Child: Needs to be Addressed

- *Physical Signs:* Like pregnancy, infection, genital bleeding or injury to genital area that proves or strongly suggest about some sexual activity has occurred.
- *Behavioural Signs:* Age inappropriate knowledge of sex, mental stress, attempting suicide, running away from home, prostitution etc. That means warning signs in children should be noticed[16].
- *Disclosure by Victimised Child:* If child discloses any signs and telling about his experiences, that should be addressed properly by adults.

Conclusion

The first and foremost thing that is to be done in curbing such offences is to have a proper legislation on child sexual abuse, which has been treated under adult laws till now. The Bill which is pending in the Parliament should come in to force so as to reduce the prevalence of the offence and also to have a deterrent affect among the abusers. The problem of child abuse needs to be curbed at root level. The first step towards it could be spreading awareness in children by providing sex education in schools and understanding the psyche of the victim.

Notes

1. 'World Health Organisation Definition of Child Abuse' <*http://www.yesican.org/definitions/WHO.html*> accessed on 13 February 2011.
2. 'Child Sexual Abuse', United States Department of Veterans Affairs, 2007 <*http://www.ptsd.va.gov/public/pages/child-sexual-abuse.asp*> accessed 12 February 2011.
3. Dr. Lovleen Kacker, Srinivas Varadan, Pravesh Kumar,' Study on Child Abuse: India 2007', Ministry of Women and Child Development, Government of India, 2007 < *http://wcd.nic.in/childabuse.pdf*> accessed on 13 February 2011.
4. 'Over 53% children face sexual abuse: Survey', *The Times of India,* New Delhi 2007, 5.
5. Laura Hoyano, Caroline Keenan, *Child Abuse Law and Policy Across Boundaries,* (1st edn, Oxford, New York 2007) 15.
6. *Ibid.*, p. 17.
7. Kirthi Jaykumar, 'Child Sexual Abuse', <*http://www.fight-back.net/lawyer_Child_Sexual_Abuse_Kirthi_Jayakumar.html*> accessed 10 February 2011.
8. Eileen Munro, '*Child Protection*', (1st edn., Sage, London, 2007), 104-105.
9. States Parties shall take all appropriate legislative, administrative, social and educational measures to protect the child from all forms of physical or mental violence, injury or abuse, neglect or negligent treatment, maltreatment or exploitation, including sexual abuse, while in the care of parent(s), legal guardian(s) or any other person who has the care of the child.
10. No one shall be subjected to torture or to inhuman or degrading treatment or punishment.
11. Paula Case, *Compensating Child Abuse in England and Wales,* (1st edn., Cambridge, 2007), 3.
12. Section 372 Whoever sells, lets to hire, or otherwise disposes of any 1 [person under the age of eighteen years with intent that such person shall at any age be employed or used for the purpose of prostitution or illicit intercourse with any person or for any unlawful and immoral purpose, or knowing it to be likely that such person will at any age be] employed or used for any such purpose, shall be punished with imprisonment of either description for a term which may extend to ten years, and shall be liable to fine.

    Section 373 Whoever buys, hires or otherwise obtains possession of any [1][person under the age of eighteen years with intent that such person shall at any age be employed or used for the purpose of prostitution or illicit intercourse with any person or for any unlawful and immoral purpose, of knowing it to be likely that such person will at any age be] employed or used for any purpose, shall be punished with imprisonment of either description for a term which may extend to ten years, and shall also be liable to fine.

    Section 375 A man is said to commit "rape" who, except in the case hereinafter excepted, has sexual intercourse with a woman under circumstances falling under any of the six following descriptions: First. Against her will. Secondly. Without her consent. Thirdly.- With her consent, when her consent has been obtained by putting her or any person in whom she is interested in fear of death or of hurt.

Fourthly. With her consent, when the man knows that he is not her husband, and that her consent is given because she believes that he is another man to whom she is or believes herself to be lawfully married. Fifthly. With her consent, when, at the time of giving such consent, by reason of unsoundness of mind or intoxication or the administration by him personally or through another of any stupefying or unwholesome substance, she is unable to understand the nature and consequences of that to which she gives consent. Sixthly. With or without her consent, when she is under sixteen years of age.

Section 377 Whoever voluntarily has carnal intercourse against the order of nature with any man, woman or animal, shall be punished with imprisonment for life, or with imprisonment of either description for term which may extend to ten years, and shall also be liable to fine.

13. Section 21, Juvenile Justice (Care and Protection of Children) Amendment Act, 2000.
14. Law Commission, 'Review of Rape Laws' 2000.
15. *Ibid.*
16. Eileen Munro, '*Child Protection*', (1st edn., Sage, London, 2007), 104-105.

POLICIES AND FRAMEWORK TO PREVENT CHILD ABUSE IN STREET CHILDREN: AN INDIAN PERSPECTIVE[1]

Shiv Shrutika[*] *& Vandana Jaiswal*[*]

> *"A world which abandons its children in the streets has no future; it no longer renders it possible to create and develop a project of life.... A world which tries to ignore the precariousness of the human condition inspires no confidence.... It is a world wherein each one survives amongst a complete spiritual disintegration. It is a world that has become simply dehumanized, and which today needs urgently to awake to the true values."*
>
> - JUDGE A. A. CANCADO TRINDADE, THE INTER-AMERICAN COURT OF HUMAN RIGHTS[2]

Introduction

"Everyone has the right to a standard of living adequate for the health and well-being of himself and of his family, including food, clothing, housing and medical care and necessary social services, and the right to security in the event of unemployment, sickness, disability, widowhood, old age or other lack of livelihood in circumstances beyond his control."[3]

UNICEF (1988), describes street children in the following manner: The term denotes not only a place of congregation, but also a certain set of working and living conditions. The vast majorities are on the street to make a living for their families and/or themselves. For these children, the street is, above all, a work place. Second, they spend large amounts of time on the street frequently because of the low returns on their labour. Third, most make their way into the informal sector as petty hawkers, shoe-shine boys, scavengers of raw materials or even thieves and street prostitutes. Fourth, by the

* Students. B.A., L.L.B. (Hons.), Semester- 6th, 3rd Year, Dr. Ram Manohar Lohiya National Law University, Lucknow, (shrutika.shiv@gmail.com) (vandanajaiswal09@gmail.com)

nature of their work and life, they are normally on their own, largely unprotected by adults.[4]

Tens of millions of children live in the streets of cities scattered all over the world. While their presence may be noticed in developed as well as developing countries, however, the majority of street children live in the poor nations of Africa, Asia, and Latin America, especially India and Brazil. Some estimates put the number of street children living in India's six most populous cities at 500,000; more than 100,000 may be found in Delhi alone. War, poverty, urbanization, rapid economic growth, the breakdown of families, and domestic violence are the most immediate causes of this phenomenon's growing proportions. Children are often more vulnerable to the devastating effects of their countries' political and economic crises; their governments often fail to provide effective protection or adequate material support. If some children are lured to the streets by the exciting prospect of being completely free, most are driven there by despair. In most cases, they simply have nowhere else to go.[5]

Issues of the Street Children

The issues and needs of the children living and working on the streets of cities have attracted widespread international and national attention. There is no doubt that the most effective response to this is prevention through general support to families in poverty, creating broad-based awareness among the parents and society, addressing the factors underlying family disintegration that propel children into a life on the streets. In addition other preventive measures required are employment for adults, support in times of crisis, strong childcare programmes, relevant schooling and efforts to address the roots of domestic violence to keep families intact so that they fulfil responsibilities towards their children.

At the same time children already on the street cannot be ignored and their rights must be vigorously defended. They need psychological support, relationships and a role in society along with the basic issues related to their survival, security, and protection from a full range of civil rights such as food, money, shelter, clothes, healthcare, education, etc. They have the right like all other children to live in dignity, to health and education, to protection from abuse and to voice their own feelings and sufferings (Article 2 and 3 of the U.N. Convention on the Rights of the Child).[6]

Analysis of Street Child Assistance in India

Until 1993, the term "street child" did not figure in the "Official Vocabulary" of post-independence India. Under pressure from the NGO's in the field of assistance to street children, both local and international, the Government of India set up a "Scheme for Assistance to Street Children" under Ministry of Welfare, which was launched in February of 1993. The Scheme was to be implemented in only six major cities initially.

There were many meetings between NGO's and Government officers prior to the release of the Scheme, and many suggestions for improvement and better management for the scheme were agreed to and noted by the Government, but not implemented in the final draft. leaving the Scheme empty and ineffective for NGO participation.

Immediately after the release, and although clearly stated three years minimum experience in the field was a requirement, it was seen that many NGO's not working in the field of street children, but with political clout, applied for and received the large amounts granted for said assistance.

Since, the programme has been extended to more cities (with 1 million plus population). But the most sincere NGO's in the field have not requested the funding because of the lack of understanding of the Government towards the assistance to street children and the flexibility needs of the NGO's in working with the street children. The jumping on the bandwagon by unqualified NGO's however, continues. There is no other scheme of assistance offered by the Government specifically for street children.

Existing Laws Concerning Street Children

There is absolutely no legislature that specifies the term "Street Children" in the judiciary of India. The laws applicable under the Juvenile Justice Act 1986 relate quite strongly to the care of and rights of street children in general, without mentioning them in any term, but are found, on a national level, not to be implemented properly at all. In fact, many police officers/constables in the field do not know about the details of the Act.

Juvenile Boards and Courts

The Juvenile Justice System has proved to be ineffective in coping with the problem under its present structure. [Example: 3,301 cases were brought before Juvenile Court in Mumbai in 1989, the number of street children is 50,000]. There are many States in India where there exists no Juvenile Board or Juvenile Court system.

Street children are, in many cases, sent to remand in adult jails where they are abused, both physically and sexually, for indefinite periods of time. There is little or no provision made for these young children to contact their parents or obtain proper guidance or legal representation. The children eventually escape from these "Homes" just as they run away from their real home. In many States, street children are placed under the "care" of observation homes, remand homes and other Government juvenile centres, but it is just as well known that these so-called child care centres are sadly lacking any semblance of actual care.

There is a need for these centres to be taken over and run by the NGO's, and the Ministry has recently mooted such a proposal for Social Welfare.

Discussions and meetings are under progress, but when the reality of such a proposal will be realised is very unclear.

The Juvenile Justice Act has to be looked at very carefully in terms of street children and needs to be closely scrutinised. If changes are affected, then the implementation of the Act on a national level needs to be seriously and permanently looked at.[7]

United Nations International Children's Educational Fund (UNICEF)

UNICEF acknowledges the need to advocate the implementation of the Convention on the Rights of the Child in India ad promote compulsory education. A number of international seminars, symposia, workshops and conferences were organised or supported by UNICEF highlighting the problems of illiteracy among the children. UNICEF in India initiated curriculum programmes and supply of books for children. It funded studies identifying situational analysis of street children in major cities of India. Currently UNICEF is supporting the Bal Adhikar Paryojana Programmes providing need based education to children out-of-schools in the carpet-weaving belt of Mirzapur and Bhadhoi.[8]

United Nations Educational, Scientific, and Cultural Organization (UNESCO)

UNESCO has been actively working for street children in India since the 1990 World Conference on Education for All, in Jomtien and the World Declaration on Education for All. The UNESCO's Education Programme for Children in need has enabled the organization to provide substantial funding and technical support for educational activities in favour of children in difficult circumstances. At the World Education Forum held in Dakar in April, 2000 UNESCO has been mandated as a lead agency supported by the official partners for promoting and ensuring the education.

Within the Framework of Education for All, UNESCO has been supporting CINI ASHA and Don Bosco Ashalayam, NGOs based in Calcutta since 1997 on a framework of programmes to meet basic needs of street and working children's survival, growth and development. The active support from UNESCO has contributed significantly in providing rehabilitation and education for street and working children in Kolkata's urban agglomeration. UNESCO is also supporting Prayas, a Delhi-based NGO in preparing a project to develop innovative educational material to accomplish the need of street and working children for education in urban surroundings.[9]

Convention on the Rights of the Child (CRC)

The Convention on the Rights of the Child is universal in its applicability to children and adolescents. The Convention defines a child as being under 18 years of age unless majority is attained earlier according to the law of the country. The Convention gives four guiding principles that are important in interpreting the rights it encompasses. These are: non-discrimination (Art. 2), best interests of the child (Art. 3), right to survival and development (Art.6), and respect for the views of the child (Art. 12). The guiding principles outlined above are necessary for the meaningful realization of all other rights.[10]

Conclusion

The world of children may be as complex as that of adults. Children should not be working for a living, but if they are (and until one can ensure that they are not involved in exploitative work), one needs to find innovative ways of protecting their other rights, such as the right to education, adequate health care and shelter, and protection from abuse and exploitation. While evolving strategies for the rehabilitation of street children one must understand their case histories and the assessment of their situation. Reasons for being on the street vary with each child. The sense of freedom may be intensely important to many of these children. Depriving them of this freedom may exacerbate matters especially when a child has strong ties to a group of peers. This involves establishing a relationship of trust with them and providing them with a safe and supportive atmosphere. Institutionalisation is definitely not the solution. Strategy has to be integrated with other services on the street.[11]

Notes

1. The authors are Shiv Shrutika and Vandana Jaiswal, 3rd Year Students of Dr. Ram Manohar Lohiya National Law University, Lucknow.
2. *Villagran Morales v. Guatemala,* Series C No. 77 (Para. 60). 43.
3. Universal Declaration of Human Rights, article 25, par. 1.
4. Shelter Don Bosco, "The World of Street Children" *http://www.shelterdonbosco.org/street.htm* accessed on 10th February 2011.
5. Federico Ferrara and Valentina Ferrara, "The Children's Prison: Street Children and India's Juvenile Justice System" *http://www.careshareindia.org/Pages/OH/OHEnglish.pdf* accessed on 10th February 2011.
6. V.K. Dewan, "Child Labour : A Socio- Legal Perspective", (1st Indian Edition, Delhi, 2009), p. 88.
7. N. S. Manihara, "Street Children", *http://www.skcv.com/street%20children%20in%20india.htm* accessed on 12th February 2011.
8. V.K. Dewan, "Child Labour : A Socio- Legal Perspective", (1st Indian Edition, Delhi, 2009), p. 101.
9. *Ibid.*, p. 102.
10. "Towards a Better Tomorrow", *http://www.searo.who.int/LinkFiles/Towards_a_Better_Tomorrow_1.pdf* accessed on 13th February 2011.
11. V.K. Dewan, "Child Labour : A Socio- Legal Perspective" (1st Indian Edition, Delhi, 2009), p. 90.

References

Ewelukwa, Uche U. (2011), "Litigating the Rights of Street Children in Regional or International Fora: Trends, Options, Barriers and Breakthroughs", *http://www.highbeam.com/doc/1G1-149613559.html* accessed on 10th February 2011.

Shelter Don Bosco (2011), "The World of Street Children" *http://www.shelterdonbosco.org/street.htm* accessed on 10th February 2011.

V. K. Dewan (2009), "Child Labour: A Socio-Legal Perspective" (1st Indian Edition, Delhi, 2009).

Federico Ferrara and Valentina Ferrara, "The Children's Prison: Street Children and India's Juvenile Justice System", *http://www.careshareindia.org/Pages/OH/OHEnglish.pdf* accessed on 10th February 2011.

Towards a Better Tomorrow", *http://www.searo.who.int/LinkFiles/Towards_a_Better_Tomorrow_1.pdf* accessed on 13th February 2011.

INDEX

D